闽菜 湘菜

湘菜 徽菜 苏菜

菜 鲁菜 粤菜 川

徽菜 鲁菜 粤菜

菜 闽菜 湘菜 徽

湘菜 徽菜 浙菜

菜 粤菜 川菜 苏

菜 徽菜 鲁菜 粤

包子家族
BAO FAMILY
COOKBOOK

RECIPES FROM THE EIGHT CULINARY REGIONS OF CHINA

CÉLINE CHUNG
& TEAM

Photographs by Grégoire Kalt
Styling by Agathe Hernandez
Artistic direction by Atelier Choque Le Goff
Preface by Catherine Roig

Interlink Books

An imprint of Interlink Publishing Group, Inc.
Northampton, Massachusetts

I DEDICATE THIS BOOK
IN PARTICULAR TO BILLY PHAM,
WHO IS BY MY SIDE IN MAKING
MY DREAMS A REALITY,
AND TO ALL OUR CHEFS
WHO HAVE SHARED THEIR
FAVORITE RECIPES.

A SPECIAL MENTION
TO THE CHUNG FAMILY,
MY FATHER RUI YAO CHUNG,
MY MOTHER XIANXUE CHUNG,
AND MY BROTHER CHRISTIAN
CHUNG, WHO TAUGHT ME
TO ENJOY THE DISHES OF
OUR CUISINE, SHARE OUR
TABLES, AND LOOK AFTER
THE STOMACHS
AND HEALTH OF THOSE
WHO ARE DEAR TO US.
THEY HAVE TAUGHT
ME THAT THE REAL WAY
TO THE HEART IS THROUGH
THE STOMACH.

包子家族

Just the right combination of talent and energy was needed to reinvent Chinese restaurants in Paris. It also took boldness to face the most appalling stereotypes of Chinese cuisine head on. Céline Chung brings all this to the table as well as one more special ingredient: her bicultural identity. Born in Paris, but from Wenzhou (south of Shanghai), she is the epitome of today's global citizen. The kind of young woman that success stories are made of on the big screen. Brilliant, determined, creative, multilingual, and community minded, Céline turns everything she touches to gold … and she is just getting started! So far she has created casual dining at Petit Bao, bringing a Parisian touch to Shanghai xiao long bao (or XLB), while Gros Bao's red-accented décor is perfect for enjoying the most delectable of Chinese specialties, such as Sichuan mapo tofu, sheng jian bao, or Peking duck. Céline discovered these delicacies when she traveled through China as a business school student, taking her back to her roots and with a single goal: to eat! As with any self-respecting Chinese family, for the Chungs, food is a religion, where love is demonstrated not through words but through cooking. Daily. Generously. Sublimely.

Céline returned with her head bursting with feelings, memories, and inspiration, her entrepreneurial spirit calling her to create the kind of Chinese restaurant that didn't yet exist in Paris. A restaurant that was neither an overpriced palace nor a hole-in-the-wall that can't tell the difference between a spring roll and a dim sum. Just a relaxed, delicious, modern place for everyone. If Gros Bao's phenomenal popularity is anything to go by, this vision has clearly been a success: you'll need to come armed with patience to get a table. Like many, I waited patiently. And in the weeks that followed, I couldn't stop thinking about the melt-in-your-mouth eggplants and their secret sauce, the scallion pancakes, the charsiu bao, and many other dishes that made me want to meet Céline and her team: Lucy, Diana, Jessica, Carole, Billy, and the others. Meeting them is like biting into a sweet chile—it's an explosion of spice and heat, but in a graceful and subtle way. Just like their cooking that you will discover in this book, they are full of joy and happiness. The cherry on top of the bao: many recipes are easy, dispelling preconceived ideas about Chinese cuisine, or rather Chinese cuisines. *Xie xie* and long live the Bao Family!

Catherine Roig

包子家族

引言
INTRODUCTION

包子家族的主厨
THE BAO FAMILY CHEFS

食材和工具
INGREDIENTS & UTENSILS

早饭
BREAKFAST

小吃
APPETIZERS

引言

INTRO-DUCTION

9

包子家族

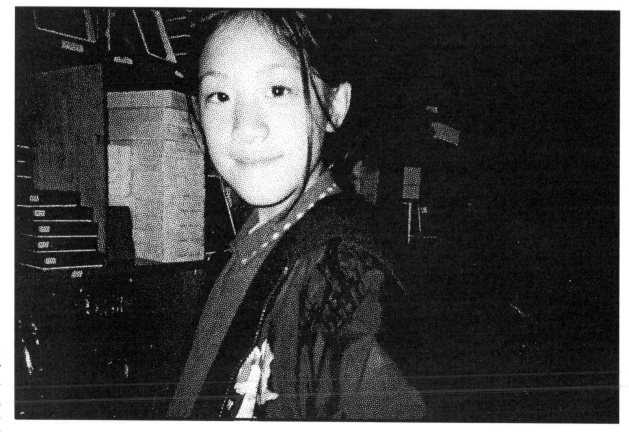

包子家族

包子家族

COOKING, OUR LOVE LANGUAGE, BY CÉLINE CHUNG

FRANCO-CHINESE CULTURE

China and France are intertwined parts of my story. I was actually born in Paris, but both my parents are from China. My father arrived in France when he was sixteen and my mother joined him at the age of nineteen, just after their marriage. At home, my mother spoke the dialect of Wenzhou, our home town (a city in Zhejiang province, south of Shanghai), while my father spoke French to us.

It was my grandfather who first settled in France. After a series of odd jobs, he managed to save enough money for his family to make a decent living. He opened ETS Chung, a leather goods store located in the Marais district on rue Saint-Merri, in the heart of Paris.

We lived in Paris, in the 3rd district, and then at my grandfather's house in Bry-sur-Marne (to the east of Paris). My mother, who had learned to cook along-side my grandmother, prepared traditional meals for lunch and dinner. The cusine of Zhejiang province is mild and slightly sweet, uses soy sauce and Shaoxing wine as a base, and is mainly comprised of vegetables and steamed fish. My mother's favorite dish was steamed sea bass with soy sauce, sprinkled with ginger and scallions.

Up until the age of ten, I had only tasted my mother's cooking. It was at this age that I discovered the cafeteria at elementary school, which opened up another world to me. One of bread, fries, macaroni, and yogurt! And when I invited my friends home, it was their turn to discover a whole new world. They learned to eat with chopsticks and were amazed by all the flavors they tasted for the first time.

At that point, what I knew about Chinese culture (and cooking) was what I had learned from my family members.

A FRESH LOOK AT CHINESE CULTURE AND CUISINE

At the age of twenty, I had an irrepressible desire to discover China with my own eyes; to get away from the vision my parents had passed on to me and to form my own view of this country and this culture that I actually knew little about. As part of my business school studies, I chose to do a university exchange in Shanghai. It was the ideal opportunity to perfect my Mandarin, live like a local, discover the country and, most importantly, experience the diversity of its cuisine!

I was swept up in curiosity and excitement as soon as I moved to Shanghai. I wandered through the streets, all my senses on the lookout ... I meandered through the city, intoxicated by the smells of food that filled the alleys from morning to evening, between the hole-in-the-wall restaurants and the fruit and vegetable stands in the middle of the street, surrounded by Chinese people walking around holding something to eat, even striding through the halls of the subway with their bags of take-out food. Food was everywhere! I set out to taste everything from breakfast to dinner, testing out all kinds of restaurants in Shanghai. It was a real culinary awakening! I also had the opportunity to travel to other parts of China: Yunnan, Sichuan, Beijing, Guangzhou, and Hong Kong. Each has its own cultural and culinary identity. Flavors, ingredients, and cooking methods differ in each region. This means that you can't talk about Chinese cuisine, but rather Chinese cuisines.

包子家族

包
子
家
族

CHINESE CUISINE: A WAY OF LIFE

Chinese cuisines are complex, flavorful, full of textures, sweet, salty, sour, and spicy; so delicious, yet so little known. Certain ingredients are favored depending on the season, and Chinese medicine traditions are respected. Food holds a key place because it defines the rhythm of the day.

As a child, I had the opportunity to visit my grandparents in China, in their native village of Wenzhou. The days consisted mainly of going to eat noodles in the morning at the hole-in-the-wall on the shopping street, $2 for a comforting bowl of hot noodles; then we would head to the market to buy vegetables and meat to prepare lunch and dinner. Afterwards, it took over an hour to cook all the dishes to be shared for lunch and then we feasted on them for at least two hours. There was Peking duck, stir-fried vegetables, noodles, steamed fish, and fruit on the table. In the afternoon, we played and ran around the courtyard of the house or had a nap, waiting for evening and dinnertime. Ultimately, the day revolved around the meals and nothing else. As a child, I didn't understand this rhythm. I found that every day was the same, it bored me, and I had the impression that life was only about eating. Growing up, I realized that meals are everything in a Chinese family, the ultimate proof of love. Meals represent a time when we care for others, show them our love—a time for sharing, exchanging ideas, having great conversations, and making decisions. Cooking in China means more than just eating, it's a way of life!

BAO FAMILY: A BRIDGE BETWEEN TWO CULTURES, BETWEEN TRADITION AND MODERNITY

When I finished my studies, I started a run-of-the-mill consulting career. I soon got bored and realized that what I was doing had no meaning for me. I had always wanted to do something entrepreneurial that was close to my heart. When I started thinking about it, the Chinese restaurant idea took hold and I immediately knew it was what I had to do. When I returned from Shanghai, my only desire was to rediscover the cuisine I had tasted there, in a place where I could spend special moments with my loved ones. But I couldn't find this place, and that's how the idea to create the restaurant of my dreams was born! It would serve authentic traditional Chinese cuisine with classic dishes, from French-sourced products as much as possible, in a modern setting with design inspired by Paris and Shanghai. I wanted to reproduce the art and way of eating in China: tables filled with communal plates, where everyone tastes and shares each dish.

Bao would be the star product, because it's timeless and requires great skill to make. It's also perfect to eat at any time of day, whether you're hungry or not! Most importantly, I wanted to break with the unfashionable clichéd image of this cuisine and make it center stage and for everyone.

We opened Petit Bao in January 2019, on rue Saint-Denis in the 2nd district, just a stone's throw from the area where I grew up. We took over a Chinese deli and it was like returning to my childhood and adding our own modern touch. It was all about respecting traditions and bringing them up to date for our lifestyle. Respecting the kitsch hallmarks that we love, and giving them a contemporary feel. Gros Bao, our second restaurant, located on the Canal Saint-Martin in the 10th district, embodies this concept completely. It is this fusion of tradition and modernity that drives us daily, in our cooking, our spaces, and our visual identity.

包
子
家
族

包子家族

FROM RESTAURANT TO COOKBOOK

I wanted to open restaurants because I wanted to bring happiness to as many people as possible. Our days can sometimes be difficult, but when you eat something good, it puts a smile on your face and brings you back to what matters most: enjoying yourself, sharing time with your loved ones, awakening your senses, and traveling. Chinese cuisine is a sharing cuisine, so Bao Family is a sharing project. We share everything we love to make you happy and transport you to China in our restaurants. And now you can travel in your own home too! These recipes have been created and adapted by our chefs so that you can explore China, from breakfast to dinner.

The real way to the heart is through the stomach!

包子家族

包子家族

LUCY CHEN

Chinese cuisine is generous but doesn't waste anything. It shows a fierce willingness to respect traditional techniques but often in unorthodox ways. It's a cuisine where years of preparation are necessary to master a technique that takes just a minute to execute. It's hearing at the same time: "You should really pay attention to your weight," and, "Please, have a little more." But above all, Chinese cuisine is undivided dedication!

It was only after cooking with chefs from around the world that I realized that these apparent contradictions are in fact characteristics of Chinese chefs, characteristics that also come through in their cooking. When I'm in a Chinese kitchen, I can clearly hear the sound of garlic and ginger cooking in a perfectly seasoned wok. I can feel steam escaping from the bamboo baskets on my face. And when I finally sit down at the table to eat, I can taste the special flavors that are the soul of this cuisine that I love so much, a soul I'm convinced will survive the test of time and changes to recipes and techniques.

包子家族

LESLIE CHIRINO

For me, Chinese cuisine is about respect. Respect for a culture so rich and different from mine, for its ingredients, and for the people I work alongside daily in the restaurant. It's also about challenges, discovering new flavors and combinations every day, and trying new techniques. But above all, it's about always seeking to learn and grow. For me, this is a pivotal part of my passion for food and cooking.

包子家族

JESSICA CHAN

I see Chinese food first and foremost as comfort and nostalgia. My grandparents are Hakka people from the Guangdong province who migrated to Hong Kong in the 1950s. Growing up, Cantonese and Hakka food was a big part of my life. My grandparents loved to cook. Food brought everyone around the table to share stories from their day at work and school. Chinese food to me means family, community, and gathering.

Chinese food now also represents adventure and discovery for the senses: sights, smells, tastes, and even sounds make up these exciting culinary experiences. I love the diversity and long history behind the cuisine. China covers a vast geographical area, and each region has its own identity with unique flavor profiles, characterized by the meats, vegetables, condiments, and sauces that are special to the terroir of each place.

Lastly, Chinese food is resourceful and humble. I admire that recipes are created to respect produce and ingredients by using every part of them. The cuisine reflects the creativity and spirit of its people.

包子家族

包子家族

LIMING SHU

《中餐》是中华民族的具有独特风味的饮食文化；是渊源流长的中华五千多年的文明历史的宝贵遗产！如今, 它融合了古今中外的烹饪精华, 深受国内外朋友的追捧和青睐！成为世界饮食文化宝库中的一颗璀璨的明珠！

其色、香、味均应具全的饮食荟萃而风靡全球！

君若未尝, 乃生平一憾！

"Chinese cuisine" is an essential and unique part of Chinese culture. It's a precious heritage made up of five thousand years of civilization and history! Nowadays, Chinese cuisine combines the essence of traditional cuisine with foreign cuisines, ancient customs, and modern practices. It's highly sought after and appreciated all over the world. With its wide range of flavors, colors, and scents, it is a shining pearl among the treasures of international culinary culture. If you haven't tasted it yet, you might regret it all your life!

VICTOR ZHENG

With the agricultural revolution, people became more sedentary and started relying on each other to source food. But they never stopped migrating, traveling away from their childhood homes, and moving to other countries. When they move away, they seek to preserve the legacy of their ancestors. They try to reproduce what is familiar to them and take new ingredients with them. All this leads to boundless creativity and culinary diversity.

Every time I ask myself where I come from, I also set out to find the origin of the flavors. The smell coming from the kitchen, the ingredients lined up on the bench, or the utensils hanging on the wall. Cooking taught me Chinese ethics, the philosophy of well-being, and the aesthetics of cooking. I grow up, I love, I leave, and I find myself.

In the end, I chose to be a chef to make the connection between food and home. For me, eating together as a family is the simplest desire of all Chinese people. And no matter where I am, I can always recall the flavors of home, of my apartment in China.

包子家族

包子家族

TENZIN

Chinese food to me is one of the healthiest around. It must be fresh, with lots of vegetables. Many of the ingredients serve medicinal purposes. Chinese meals are shared communally, with dishes placed in the center of the table, friends and family seated around with their rice bowls. You'll rarely see a knife and fork at a Chinese table as they use chopsticks instead. How do they cut meat? No need to, ingredients are prepared bite-sized and ready-to-eat with chopsticks. In China, every province has its own culinary traditions. These traditions, combined with the number of cooking methods that exist (steaming, stewing, stir-frying, roasting), mean that ingredients in Chinese cuisine can be prepared in so many ways!

MADAME CHUN

What is Chinese cuisine? There are different Chinese cuisines. Each region has a different cuisine and different flavors.

Whether they are fried, stir-fried, or simmered, all the dishes are delicious. Chinese dishes are extremely varied, they can be savory or sweet, meat-based or vegetarian, showcasing treasures of the land as well as the sea. Their colors, aromas, and tastes come together to provide a rich, rounded culinary experience. Simply put, Chinese cuisine has a long history and it is multifaceted and delicious.

包子家族

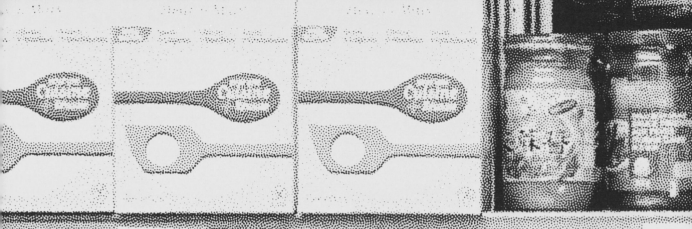

MATCHA

RICE VINEGAR

包子家族

酱料
CONDIMENTS, THICK SAUCES & PASTES

LAO GAN MA SPICY CHILE CRISP / LǍO GĀN MÁ ....老干妈

A brand of chile oil well known in China and around the world. It is made with chiles, fermented soybeans, garlic, and onions. We use it in recipes or as a condiment.

BLACK BEAN GARLIC SAUCE / SUÀN RÓNG DÒUCHǏ JIÀNG ....蒜蓉豆豉酱

A sauce made with black fermented soybeans and garlic, it can be used in stir-fried dishes or steamed dishes. It works well with seafood.

SPICY FERMENTED BEAN SAUCE OR PASTE / LÀ DÒU BÀN JIÀNG ....辣豆瓣酱

Dou ban jiang is a paste made from fermented fava beans, soybeans, and chile. It is chunky, red and brown in color, and contains umami, salty, and spicy flavors. It is widely used in the cuisine of the Sichuan region. For example, oil is heated in the wok, then dou ban jiang is added and fried as a base for mapo tofu sauce.

SWEET FERMENTED BEAN SAUCE / TIÁN MIÀN JIÀNG ....甜面酱

A dark, thick sauce that mainly contains fermented wheat flour and sometimes soybeans, contrary to what its name might suggest. It is often used for making zhajiang mian, and adds a sweet, salty, and umami taste.

SESAME PASTE / ZHĪ MA JIÀNG ....芝麻酱

Unlike tahini, which uses raw white sesame seeds, this sesame paste is made with toasted sesame seeds. It is therefore darker and has a richer flavor. It is used in sauces for cold noodles or as a base for sauces served with Chinese hot pot.

HOISIN SAUCE / HǍIXIĀN JITO NG ....海鲜酱

This thick and dark fermented soybean paste is commonly used in Cantonese cuisine in marinades for rotisseries or simply as a sauce served alongside Peking duck.

CONDENSED MILK / LIÀNRǓ ....炼乳

Smooth and sweet, it is often used in drinks, such as Hong Kong milk tea, or in desserts.

FERMENTED BLACK BEANS / DÒUCHǏ ....豆豉

Fermented whole dried black soybeans are used as a base for fermented soy sauce, but they can also be used whole in sautéed or braised dishes.

FERMENTED YELLOW SOYBEAN PASTE / HUÁNGDÒU JIÀNG ....黄豆浆

A sauce made from fermented yellow soybeans. It is widely used in the Beijing area and in northern Chinese cuisine. It is used in particular in the preparation of zhajiang mian.

酱汁
LIQUID CONDIMENTS

包子家族

SESAME OIL / ZHĪ MA YÓU ....芝麻油

Sesame oil can be made from toasted or untoasted sesame seeds. Toasted seeds add a lot of flavor to dishes, which is why we prefer to use this oil. It can be used in marinades or added at the end of cooking, as it should not be heated too much.

RICE VINEGAR / MI CÙ .... 米醋

A clear colorless vinegar made from fermented rice that is quite mild and not as potent as a white vinegar. It can be used to add acidity to stir-fried dishes or sauces.

YONGCHUN VINEGAR /
YǑNGCHŪN LǍO CU ....永春老醋

Black vinegar made from fermented glutinous rice, used for marinating cold dishes, preparing braised dishes, or simply as a dipping sauce for dumplings. Chinkiang is another popular black vinegar.

OYSTER SAUCE / HÁO YÓU .... 蚝油

A dark-colored sauce with a thick texture. Oyster sauce is mainly used in Cantonese cuisine and adds flavor and umami to dishes. It is used in marinades and sauces or in stir-fried dishes.

LIGHT SOY SAUCE / SHĒNG CHŌU .... 生抽

Light soy sauce is a key ingredient in Chinese cuisine. It has a light color and liquid texture and is used to salt and season dishes.

DARK SOY SAUCE / LǍO CHŌU .... 老抽

Dark soy sauce is darker, has a more syrupy texture, and is also slightly sweeter than light soy sauce. As it is less salty, it is mainly used to add color to dishes.

SHAOXING WINE/
SHÀO XĪNG HUĀ DIĀO JIU ....紹興花雕酒

Chinese rice wine originally from Shaoxing city in the Zhejiang province. It is made by fermenting rice with water and a little wheat. There are several types—some are consumed directly as alcohols (those that are fermented longer) and others of lesser quality and with added salt are used for cooking. This wine adds depth and complexity to dishes. It is used in marinades or in fillings (for wontons and dumplings), during wok cooking, to deglaze and flavor sautéed dishes, or to add taste to simmered dishes.

包子家族

香料
SPICES

DRIED CHILES / GĀN LÀJIĀO .... 干辣椒

Dried whole chiles are widely used in Sichuan cuisine.

CHILE POWDER / LÀJIĀO MIÀN .... 辣椒麵

A powder made from roasted and dried chiles. It is used to add spice to dishes.

SICHUAN PEPPER / HUĀJIĀO .... 花椒

With a fresh aroma and citrus notes, Sichuan pepper comes in green and red varieties and can be used whole, toasted, or ground. Sichuan powder is used in marinades or in cooking and to add flavor to sautéed dishes. It is also what gives you a tingly, numbing sensation.

ORANGE PEEL / CHÉNPÍ .... 陳皮

Orange peel is used together with other spices to make broths, stews, and various simmered dishes.

LIQUORICE / GĀNCǍO .... 甘草

Often found in thinly sliced form, it is used in spice mixtures for flavoring things like soups.

STAR ANISE / BĀJIĀO .... 八角

Star-shaped and slightly red-brown in color, this spice adds an aniseed flavor to dishes. Be mindful to use it sparingly.

GOJI BERRIES / GǑUQǏZǏ .... 枸杞子

Goji berries have many health benefits, so they are often used in soups or hearty, nourishing dishes.

包子家族

经典食材
STAPLE INGREDIENTS

CENTURY EGGS OR 100-YEAR-OLD EGGS / PÍ DÀN .... 皮蛋

Century eggs are mostly made with duck eggs that are preserved for a few weeks, or even a few months, in a mixture that includes lime, paddy (unhusked) rice, ash, salt, and tea leaves. The egg white takes on a translucent brown color and a jelly-like texture and the yolk becomes creamy and dark green.

SALTED EGGS / XIÁNDÀN .... 咸蛋

Salted eggs can be raw or cooked and are made by soaking duck eggs in brine.

SILKEN TOFU / NÈNDÒUFU .... 嫩豆腐

Made from soybeans, silken (or soft) tofu has not been drained or pressed and still contains a lot of water.

FIRM TOFU / LĀODÒUFU .... 老豆腐

Firm tofu is drained and pressed, but still contains some water.

WOOD EAR MUSHROOMS / MÙ'ĚR .... 木耳

Mushrooms with a crunchy texture and a subtle taste that easily take on other flavors.

SHIITAKE MUSHROOMS / XIĀNG GŪ .... 香菇

Mostly found in dried form in Asian grocery stores. When they are rehydrated, strong umami flavors emerge. The soaking water is kept to prepare soups and other stews.

PICKLED MUSTARD GREENS / SUĀNCÀI .... 酸菜

Pickled mustard greens are often used in soups or stir-fried dishes. They add a lot of flavor and depth to dishes.

HULLED MUNG BEANS / LÚ DÒU .... 绿豆

Mung beans can be eaten in seed or sprouted form. When they are used as seeds, they are for making soups or sweet fillings. Once they are sprouted, they are known as bean sprouts, which are often eaten in salads or stir-fried.

BLACK SESAME SEEDS / HĒI ZHĪMA .... 黑芝麻

Sesame seeds are mostly used toasted. They are used in sweet and savory dishes and are often used as a garnish.

包子家族

包子家族

包子家族

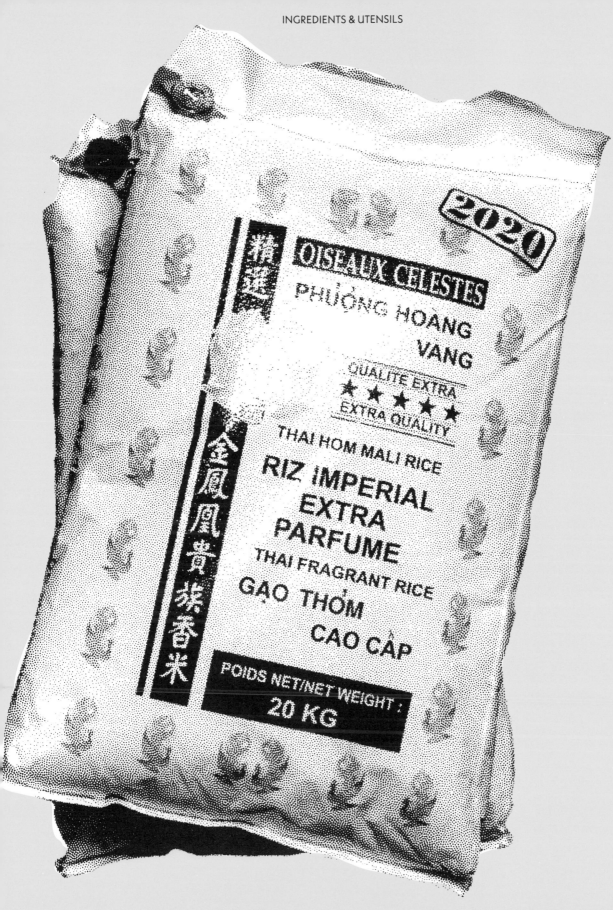

包子家族

淀粉 面粉 糖
STARCHES, FLOURS & SUGARS

WHEAT STARCH / XIĂOMÀI DIÀNFĚN ....小麦淀粉

When mixed with a liquid and heated, wheat starch becomes translucent and slightly sticky. It is mainly used in combination with rice flour and other starches to make dim sum, such as har gow or cheungfun.

POTATO STARCH / TǓDÒU DIÀNFĚN ....土豆淀粉

Used as a thickener, most commonly in the making of noodles or breadcrumb coatings.

RICE FLOUR / NIÁN MǏ FĚN ....粘米粉

Made from very finely ground rice, it is used to make rice cakes or radish cakes (luo bo gao).

GLUTINOUS (STICKY) RICE FLOUR / NUÒ MǏ FĚN ....糯米粉

Similar in appearance to rice flour, glutinous rice flour gives a sticky texture. It is used in many dim sum and dessert recipes.

TAPIOCA FLOUR / MÙ SHǓ FĚN ....木薯粉

Tapioca flour (starch) is extracted from cassava root and can be used to thicken sauces, make rice noodles or dumpling dough, or to yield the sticky and elastic texture found in desserts such as taro balls.

CANE SUGAR / ZHÈ TÁNG ....蔗糖

Minimally processed cane sugar gives dishes a more complex molasses flavor than the more refined white sugar.

ROCK SUGAR / BĪNG TANG ....冰糖

Rock sugar is sold in the form of irregular pieces that can be white or translucent yellow and it is less sweet than granulated sugar. Rock sugar can be used in savory dishes to counterbalance salt and bring flavors together or to create a glossy finish. It is also used for making desserts.

面和米
NOODLES & RICE

包子家族

RICE NOODLES / HÉFĚN .... 河粉

Wide noodles made from rice flour and tapioca or corn starch.

FINE YELLOW NOODLES/ CHÁNGSHÒU .... 长寿面

Thin wheat noodles with a yellow color that comes from turmeric.

RAMEN NOODLES / LĀMIÀN .... 拉面

Wheat noodles.

JASMINE RICE / XIĀNGMĬ .... 香米

Soft, thick, and fragrant rice grains that are often cooked in a rice cooker. Rinse the rice three times before cooking. For optimal results, to test you have used the right amount of water, the water should reach your fingertips when you place your fist onto the rice in the pot.

SWEET POTATO VERMICELLI / HÓNGSHŬ FĚNSĪ .... 红薯粉丝

Long, dark-grey vermicelli noodles that become translucent and light after cooking.

包子家族

包子家族

包子家族

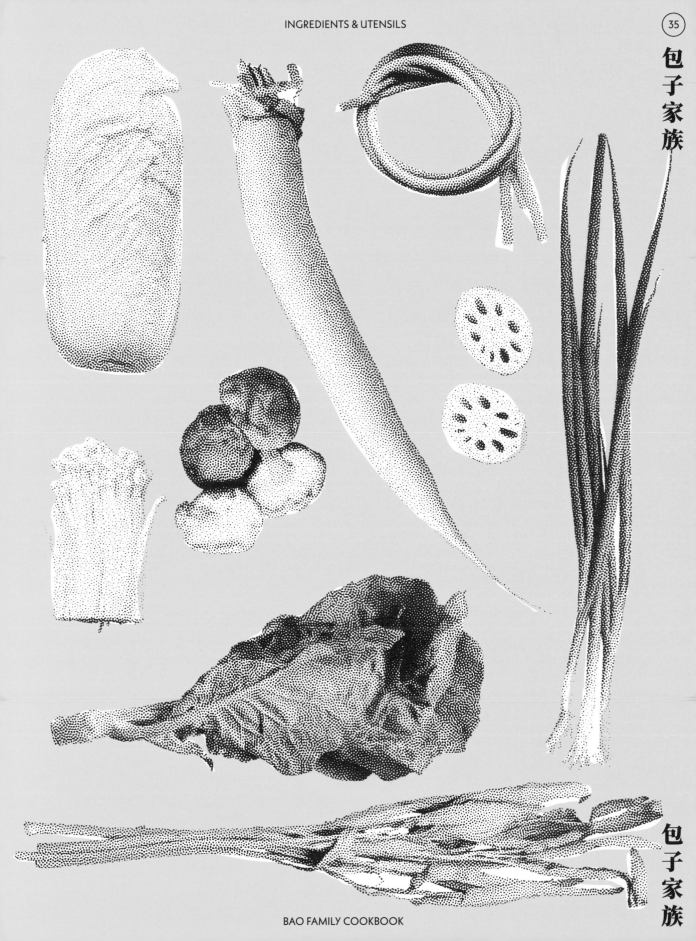

包子家族

新鲜食材
FRESH PRODUCE

LEBANESE OR JAPANESE EGGPLANTS / QIÉ ZI .... 茄子

These eggplants are longer and thinner than those usually found in the West. They should be firm and dense when purchased.

SCALLIONS / XIĀNG CŌNG .... 香葱

Scallions (spring onions) are commonly used in Chinese cuisines. They can be the main ingredient in dishes, such as scallion pancakes or Shanghai noodles, or they can be used in marinades or as a garnish.

CILANTRO / XIĀNG CÀI .... 香菜

Fresh cilantro is widely used in Chinese cuisine. It adds flavor and a hint of freshness to dishes. Both leaves and stems are used.

BEAN SPROUTS / DÒU YÁ .... 豆芽

These are often stir-fried in wok dishes together with other ingredients.

WATER SPINACH / KŌNG XĪN CÀI ....空心菜

These leafy greens have long hollow stems with small, thin dark-green leaves at the end.

CHINESE BROCCOLI / GAI LAN / JIÈ LÁN .... 芥兰

This leafy green vegetable is recognizable by its long light-green stems and wide dark-green leaves.

GARLIC CHIVES / JIǓ CÀI .... 韭菜

This delicate herb has long flat stems with a very pronounced garlic flavor and smell. They are primarily eaten cooked.

YARDLONG BEANS / JIĀNG DÒU .... 豇豆

Denser and crunchier than green beans, they are mostly stir-fried in a wok.

GARLIC SCAPES / SUÀNMIÁO .... 蒜苗

These long green young garlic shoots are often used to make a side dish.

WINTER MELON OR WAX GOURD / DŌNG GUĀ .... 冬瓜

Contrary to its name, winter melon is actually a variety of squash. It has white flesh, a very mild taste, and is mostly used in soups.

LOTUS ROOT / LIÁN ǑU .... 莲藕

The edible stem of the lotus flower. Choose firm and fresh lotus roots and wash them thoroughly before cooking.

NAPA CABBAGE OR CHINESE CABBAGE / PE-TSAÏ / DÀ BÁI CÀI .... 大白菜

Chinese cabbage has long, light-green leaves. Soft and easy to cook, it is often used in soups, stir-fries, or dumplings.

SHIITAKE MUSHROOMS / XIĀNG GŪ .... 香菇

Fresh mushrooms with a buttery flavor.

ENOKI MUSHROOMS / JĪN ZHĒN GŪ ......金针菇

Small, long, thin white mushrooms, with a crunchy texture. They are often used in stir-fries and soups.

DAIKON / LUÓ BO / MOOLI .... 萝卜

This large long white radish is mild in flavor and eaten raw or cooked. Choose heavy ones with nice green leaves.

包子家族

包子家族

中式厨房用具
BASIC UTENSILS

STEAMER BASKET / SHĀOJĪ .... 筲箕

Mainly used to steam-cook food, it can also serve as a colander, container, or even as a serving dish.

CLEAVER / CÀIDĀO .... 菜刀

An essential knife in any Chinese cuisine that can be used for almost anything. It can be made of carbon steel or stainless steel.

LADLE / GUŌ CHĂN .... 锅铲

A ladle is very useful for wok cooking. It is used to stir, pour liquids into the wok during cooking, or transfer cooked ingredients onto plates.

ROLLING PIN / GĂN MIÀN ZHÀNG .... 擀麵杖

A wooden rolling pin that is thinner than a traditional pastry rolling pin. Its shape makes it easier to hold when rolling out rounds of bao dough.

ROUND SLOTTED SKIMMER SPOON OR SPIDER / LOÙ PIÁO .... 漏瓢

This type of spoon makes it easy to remove noodles or dumplings after cooking in water or oil.

CHOPSTICKS / KUÀI ZI .... 筷子

Chopsticks are often used to mix ingredients or to separate them when frying.

METAL SPATULA / DĂ XIÀN CHĬ .... 打馅尺

A spatula is mainly used to spread dumpling or xiao long bao filling onto the dough. It is optional and you can easily use a spoon instead.

WOK / CHĂO GUŌ .... 炒鍋

A wok is another essential utensil. It is used for all stir-fried dishes, but also for frying, steaming, or boiling. Its curved base allows both the heat and ingredients to be evenly distributed. For the most part, it is made of cast iron or carbon steel. It can have a long handle, two side handles, or a long handle and a side handle, depending on its main use.

There are a number of tutorials online to learn how to season a wok before its first use, as well as what kind of tools should be used to clean it. For home use, the best method is to take the rough side of a sponge and gently rub the wok under running water with a little soap, until there is no more food on the surface. If food remains stuck or the wok is particularly greasy, you can pour hot water into it to soften the remaining food or to degrease the surface. Next, rinse it under water and dry it inside and out with a dish towel. Put the wok back on the heat to remove any remaining moisture, then turn off the heat. Use paper towel to coat the whole wok with a thin layer of vegetable oil. What to remember: ❶ Do not rub the wok too hard, just enough for the surface to be clean. ❷ It is not necessary to leave the wok over very high heat or thoroughly oil the whole surface, as may be the case in a professional kitchen. ❸ Make sure that the wok is always perfectly dry, otherwise it may rust and you will have to treat it before using it next.

包子家族

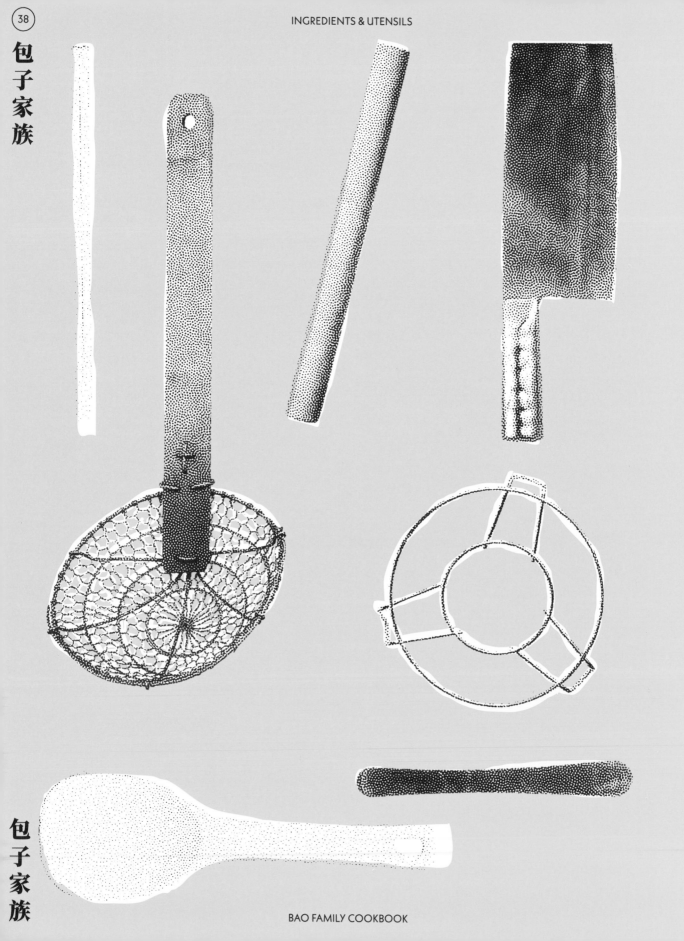

包子家族

包子家族

包子家族

包子家族

早饭

BREAKFAST
41

皮蛋瘦肉粥
CONGEE WITH CENTURY EGGS

SERVES ABOUT 5

INGREDIENTS

RICE ....2 CUPS (400 G)
WATER.................................10½ CUPS (2.5 LITERS)
PORK NECK.................................3½ OZ (100 G)
CENTURY EGGS ....3 OR 4
SALT...TO YOUR TASTE
WHITE PEPPER ....4 PINCHES
LIGHT SOY SAUCE ....A FEW DROPS
SESAME OIL................................A FEW DROPS

GARNISH
CHOPPED CILANTRO OR SCALLIONS

❶ Rinse and drain the rice and place it in a large pot. ● Pour in the water and bring to a boil, then cook, covered, over low heat for 30 minutes.

❷ Meanwhile, thinly slice the pork. Cut the century eggs into quarters and then into small pieces.

❸ Take the lid off the rice and add the pork and eggs. ● Leave to simmer for 2 to 3 minutes over medium–high heat. ● Add salt, white pepper, and soy sauce to your taste. ● Add a few drops of sesame oil, garnish with fresh cilantro or scallions, and serve.

油条
YOUTIAO
CHINESE FRIED DOUGH

MAKES AROUND 12 PIECES

INGREDIENTS

ALL-PURPOSE FLOUR .... 4 CUPS (500 G)
BAKING POWDER .... SCANT 1 TABLESPOON
SALT .... 1 TEASPOON
BAKING SODA .... ⅔ TEASPOON

EGG 1
ICE-COLD WATER .... 1⅛–1¼ CUPS (280–290 ML)
VEGETABLE OIL .... FOR OILING AND FRYING

❶ Mix the flour, baking powder, salt, and baking soda in a large bowl. ● In another bowl, whisk the egg and cold water together and gradually mix this into the dry ingredients until it comes together ● Mix until a smooth dough is obtained, cover with plastic wrap, and leave in a humid place for 1½ hours.

❷ Knead the dough until smooth, then let it rest again for an additional 45 minutes.

❸ In a pot, heat the frying oil to 350°F (180°C). ● Meanwhile, on an oiled work surface, roll out the dough to form a rectangle about ½ inch (1 cm) thick, then cut it into 1¼ × 3½ inch (3 × 9 cm) strips. ● Stack two strips on top of each other and press down firmly all the way down the length using a chopstick.

❹ Holding both ends, carefully drop each youtiao into the hot oil. ● Turn constantly for 30 seconds so that they cook evenly on all sides, then remove and transfer to paper towels to drain excess oil.

❺ These are delicious served with hot or cold soy milk.

包子家族

早饭

煎蛋饭
FRIED EGG ON RICE

WE LIKE TO USE FRIED SHALLOTS, DRIED PORK, SCALLIONS, AND SESAME SEEDS AS A GARNISH.

SERVES 1

INGREDIENTS

COOKED RICE .... **1 BOWL**
VEGETABLE OIL ....**1 TABLESPOON**
EGG **1**
SOY SAUCE .... **A DRIZZLE**

GARNISH
CHOPPED CILANTRO OR SCALLION
DRIED PORK
FRIED SHALLOTS
SESAME SEEDS

❶ Ready your bowl of rice.

❷ Heat a frying pan over medium–high heat, then pour in the oil. ● Break the egg into the pan and cover. ● When the white begins to set, remove the lid and fry until the yolk reaches the desired consistency.

❸ Serve on top of the rice with a drizzle of soy sauce and add your choice of garnish.

包子家族

果酱炸馒头
FRIED MANTOU WITH JAM

MANTOU (STEAMED BUNS) ARE STEAMED BALLS OF BAOZI DOUGH (PAGE 86) WITHOUT A FILLING, WHICH ARE USUALLY SERVED ALONGSIDE SAUCE DISHES. HERE, THEY ARE SLICED, FRIED, AND TOPPED WITH SUGAR OR JAM TO MAKE A SWEET BREAKFAST TO START YOUR MORNING. SUPER SIMPLE BUT INCREDIBLY ADDICTIVE, THIS RECIPE IS IDEAL FOR USING UP LEFTOVER BAOZI DOUGH OR DAY-OLD MANTOU.

INGREDIENTS
MANTOU
OIL FOR FRYING
JAM AND/OR CONFECTIONERS' SUGAR, TO SERVE

❶ Cut the mantou into thick slices.

❷ Heat a frying pan over medium heat and pour in a drizzle of oil. ● Place the mantou slices in the pan and allow them to toast. ● Let them cook slowly (you can press lightly on the mantou so that the whole surface browns), until they are golden.

● Turn over and repeat on the other side (add a little more oil if necessary).

❸ Serve sprinkled with sugar and/or with your favorite jam.

菠萝包
PINEAPPLE BUNS

MAKES AROUND 10 BUNS

PINEAPPLE BUNS (菠萝包 BO LUO BAO IN MANDARIN) CAN BE FOUND EVERYWHERE IN HONG KONG. DESPITE THEIR NAME, THEY DO NOT CONTAIN PINEAPPLE; THESE MILDLY SWEET BUNS ARE NAMED FOR THEIR TOP LAYER, WHICH IS SOMETIMES RIDGED AND REMINISCENT OF PINEAPPLE SKIN. PINEAPPLE BUNS ARE MOSTLY EATEN IN CHA CHAAN TENGS (HONG KONG-STYLE DINERS), AT ANY TIME OF THE DAY, EITHER PLAIN WITH A DRINK, SPREAD WITH BUTTER, OR AS A SANDWICH BUN. THERE ARE ALSO FILLED VERSIONS WITH A VARIETY OF SWEET AND SAVORY FILLINGS (LIKE CUSTARD, COCONUT, OR CHARSIU).

DOUGH	
BREAD FLOUR	1⅓ CUPS (200 G) + FOR DUSTING
WHITE SUGAR	3 TABLESPOONS
BEATEN EGG	½ TABLESPOON (RESERVE THE REST)
INSTANT YEAST	1½ TEASPOONS (3 G)
MILK	SCANT ½ CUP (100 ML)
UNSALTED BUTTER, DICED	1½ TABLESPOONS

TOP LAYER	
ALL-PURPOSE FLOUR	¾ CUP (100 G)
BAKING POWDER	¼ TEASPOON
BAKING SODA	⅛ TEASPOON
DRY MILK POWDER	2 TEASPOONS
BUTTER	4 TABLESPOONS (2 OZ)
WHITE SUGAR	¼ CUP (45 G)
BEATEN EGG	½ TABLESPOON + EXTRA TO GLAZE

DOUGH PREPARATION

❶ Place all the dough ingredients except the butter in the bowl of a stand mixer fitted with a dough hook, then knead until smooth. ● Add the diced butter and mix again until well combined. ● Cover with a dish towel and leave the dough to rest in a warm place until it doubles in volume.

❷ Place the dough on a lightly floured work surface, then press gently to knock it down.

❸ Divide the dough into 10 portions, each 1¼ to 1½ oz (35 to 40 g), cover with a damp cloth or plastic wrap, and allow to rest for 5 minutes.

❹ Form each piece of dough into a ball, space them out on a baking sheet, cover again, and leave to rise until they double in volume.

TOP LAYER

❶ Sift the flour, baking powder, baking soda, and milk powder into a bowl. ● Set aside.

❷ In another bowl, beat the butter and sugar together until creamy. ● Add the beaten egg and then gradually mix in the dry ingredients to form a smooth dough. ● Roll into a log and wrap in plastic wrap, then refrigerate for about 1 hour (or just enough time for it to firm up a little and become play-dough like in texture).

❸ Preheat the oven to 340°F (170°C). ● Divide the topping into ¾ oz (20 g) portions, place each portion between two sheets of parchment paper, and flatten with the palm of your hand (or a rolling pin).

❹ Brush each bun with beaten egg and gently place a portion of topping on top. ● Brush with egg again.

❺ Place on the bottom shelf of the oven and bake for 12 to 15 minutes, until the buns are golden brown.

小吃

APPETIZERS
55

涼拌茄子
MARINATED SPICY EGGPLANTS

SERVES 2 TO 3

INGREDIENTS
LEBANESE OR JAPANESE EGGPLANTS	1 LB 5 OZ (600 G)
OIL FOR FRYING	

MARINADE
CHOPPED GINGER	1 CUP (100 G)
MINCED GARLIC	½ CUP (100 G)
WHITE SUGAR	6 TABLESPOONS
SESAME OIL	3 TABLESPOONS
CILANTRO	1 SPRIG
CHOPPED SCALLION	2 TABLESPOONS
LEMON JUICE	SCANT 1 CUP (200 ML)
SOY SAUCE	1 CUP (240 ML)
WATER	1 CUP (240 ML)
CHILE OIL	2 TABLESPOONS

GARNISH
SESAME SEEDS	1 PINCH
FRESH RED CHILE	1
CILANTRO (OPTIONAL)	1 SMALL HANDFUL

❶ Cut the eggplants into 4 × ¾ inch (10 × 2 cm) wedges. ● Heat a 2 inch (5 cm) depth of oil in a pan until 325°F (160°C), and fry the eggplant slices until they are just cooked and their skin turns deep purple. ● Transfer to a plate lined with paper towels to drain excess oil, then allow to cool. (If you prefer a lighter version, boil the eggplants in a shallow depth of water in a pan, but their color will not be as vibrant.)

❷ Combine the marinade ingredients in a large dish and add the cooled eggplants. ● For best results, leave the eggplants to marinate for at least 5 hours.

❸ Transfer to a serving dish and garnish with sesame seeds, finely chopped fresh chile, and cilantro, if using.

淹黄瓜
MARINATED CUCUMBERS

小吃

SERVES 10

INGREDIENTS

CUCUMBER ....1 LB 2 OZ (500 G)

MARINADE

GARLIC ....2 OZ (60 G)
WHITE SUGAR ....1¼ CUPS (240 G)
RICE VINEGAR ....¾ CUP (180 ML)
SESAME OIL...⅓ CUP (90 ML)
SALT ....2½ TABLESPOONS

GARNISH

SESAME SEEDS..1 PINCH
FRESH CHILE, CHOPPED 1
CHOPPED SCALLION..1 TEASPOON

❶ Finely chop the garlic. ● Combine all the marinade ingredients and set aside.

❷ Place the cucumbers on your work surface and crush them using the handle of a knife until they break in half. ● Separate the pieces by hand and remove the seeds with a spoon. ● Use the same spoon to cut the two halves into half-moon shaped pieces, then place them all in a bowl.

❸ Pour the marinade over the cucumbers so that all the pieces are covered. ● Allow to stand for at least 1½ hours. If you prefer a lightly seasoned cucumber,

remove immediately, but you can leave the cucumber to marinate longer if you prefer more depth of flavor. Reserve the marinade.

❹ Serve the cucumber pieces with a little marinade. ● Garnish with sesame seeds, chile, and scallion.

TIP

The marinade can be reused for other cucumbers! It can also be used as a salad dressing or in a cold noodle sauce.

包子家族

小吃

葱油煎饼
CHINESE SCALLION PANCAKES

MAKES 10 PANCAKES

PANCAKE DOUGH	
ALL-PURPOSE FLOUR	**4 CUPS (500 G) + FOR DUSTING**
SALT	**¼ TEASPOON**
INSTANT YEAST	**⅔ TEASPOON (2 G)**
VEGETABLE OIL	**2 TABLESPOONS**
WATER AT 175°F (80°C)	**1 CUP (250 ML)**

FILLING	
SALT	
SESAME OIL FOR BRUSHING	
ALL-PURPOSE FLOUR FOR SPRINKLING	
SCALLIONS, CHOPPED	**3**

COOKING	
OIL FOR FRYING	

❶ Place the flour, salt, yeast, vegetable oil, and water in the bowl of a stand mixer fitted with a dough hook. ● Set the mixer at low speed for 8 minutes, or knead by hand until smooth and elastic. ● Continue mixing or kneading for another 1 to 2 minutes if necessary. ● Transfer the dough to a clean bowl. Cover loosely with plastic wrap or a slightly damp clean tea towel. ● Allow to stand at room temperature for 1 hour.

❷ Remove the dough from the bowl and knead it gently a couple of times. ● Divide the dough into two pieces, covering one half while you work with the other.

❸ Lightly flour your work surface. ● Roll each piece of dough evenly into a wide ⅛–³⁄₁₆ inch (3–4 mm) thick oval shape. ● Make sure you roll out the dough gradually and patiently.

❹ Sprinkle 3 pinches of salt on each dough oval from a height, making sure it is evenly distributed. ● Run your fingers over the surface to "feel" the seasoning of the dough. ● It should be lightly but evenly spread over the entire surface (you can always add more salt after cooking).

❺ Apply a thin layer of sesame oil to the entire surface of the dough with a pastry brush (or with your fingertips if you do not have one). ● Sprinkle a large pinch of flour onto each oval. ● Spread the chopped scallions evenly over the entire surface of the dough.

❻ Starting from the edge closest to you, gently roll each oval of dough into a tight log. ● Cut each log into 5 pieces, around 2¾ oz (80 g) each. ● Roll one piece into a rope. Pinch the ends, then twist the ends of the rope in opposite directions (as if you were wringing out a towel). Coil the rope into a round spiral, tuck in the end, and flatten a little to ensure it keeps its shape. Set aside to rest while you form the rest of the spirals. ● Roll out each spiral to a pancake with an even thickness of about ¹⁄₁₆ inch (2 mm).

❼ Heat a good glug of oil in a frying pan and fry each pancake over medium heat, until the pancake bubbles are nicely golden, the dough is cooked, and the surface is slightly golden. ● It is important that there is sufficient oil in the pan to cook both the surface and in between all the folds. ● Cut into quarters and serve.

包子家族

蛋黄焗南瓜
PUMPKIN FRIES
WITH SALTED EGG

SERVES 2

INGREDIENTS

PUMPKIN .... 1 LB 5 OZ (600 G)
SALTED DUCK EGG YOLKS 2
CORNSTARCH .... 1 TABLESPOON

VEGETABLE OIL .... 1 TABLESPOON + FOR FRYING
SHAOXING WINE .... 1 TABLESPOON
CHOPPED SCALLIONS .... 1 SMALL HANDFUL
SALT

❶ Cut the pumpkin in half and remove all the seeds. ● Place the flat surface on a cutting board and carefully remove the skin. ● Cut the pumpkin into ½ inch (1.5 cm) thick slices, then cut into wedges. ● Sprinkle the pumpkin slices with 1 teaspoon salt and set aside for at least 10 minutes so they release as much water as possible.

❷ In a small pot, steam the salted duck egg yolks for 12 minutes, then crush them with a fork.

❸ Add the cornstarch to the fries and mix so that each stick is coated. ● Heat 1 inch (2.5 cm) depth of oil in a pan until it is 325°F (160°C) and fry the pumpkin in batches for 1 to 2 minutes until the breading starts to turn nice and golden. ● Remove and transfer to paper towels to drain excess oil.

❹ In a large frying pan, heat the 1 tablespoon of vegetable oil over medium–high heat, then add the crushed egg yolks and stir. ● Pour in the Shaoxing wine and continue stirring until you have a foamy, smooth mixture. ● Add the pumpkin fries and stir to coat them in the sauce. ● Add a pinch of salt, garnish with chopped scallions, and serve.

TIP

Only the egg yolk is needed for this recipe. If you can't find already separated eggs, you can always buy whole eggs and separate the yolks from the whites.

包子家族

小吃

醉鸡
DRUNKEN CHICKEN WINGS

SERVES 2

INGREDIENTS	
GINGER	5 SLICES
GARLIC	1 CLOVE
RED ASIAN SHALLOT, CHOPPED	1
CHICKEN WINGS	10
SALT	1 TABLESPOON

SAUCE	
BEER	SCANT 1 CUP (200 ML)
BAY LEAF	1
SICHUAN RED PEPPERS	5
STAR ANISE	3
CINNAMON STICK	½
WHITE SUGAR	3 TABLESPOONS
LIGHT SOY SAUCE	3½ TABLESPOONS
GOJI BERRIES	8
SHAOXING WINE	1¼ CUPS (300 ML)

❶ Heat all the sauce ingredients except the Shaoxing wine in a saucepan, then leave to cool. ● Once the liquid has cooled, pour in the wine and set aside.

❷ Half-fill a large pot with water, bring to a boil, and add the ginger, garlic, and chopped shallot. Add the chicken wings and salt and wait for the water to start boiling again. ● Leave to simmer for 6 minutes, then turn off the heat and leave to cook, covered, for another 6 minutes, or until fully cooked. ● Remove the chicken wings and immediately immerse them in iced water (this will firm up the skin). Drain.

❸ Place the chicken wings in the sauce and leave to marinate overnight. ● Serve cold.

包子家族

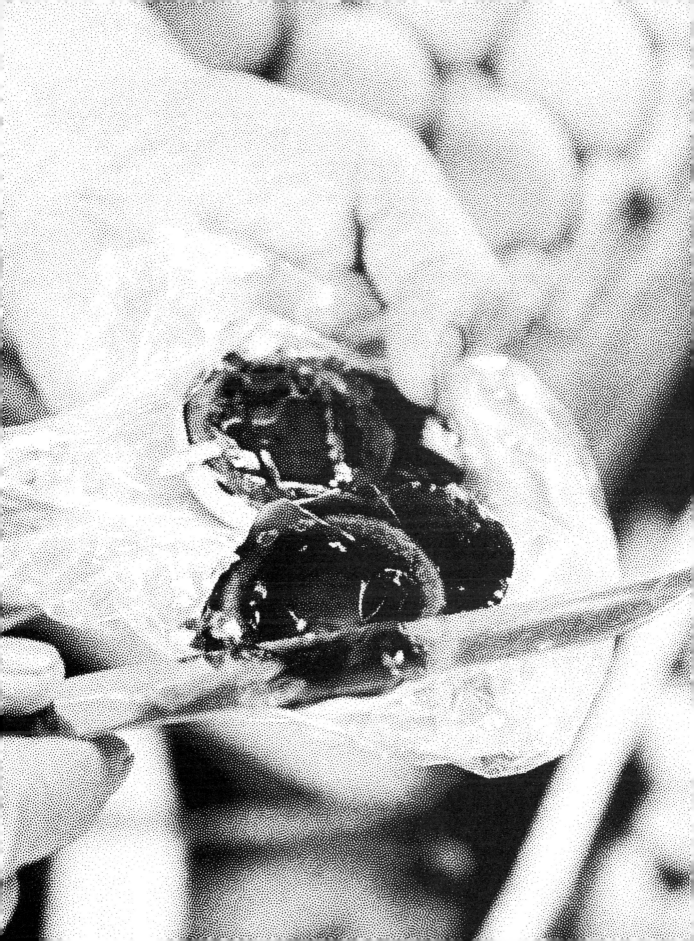

蚵仔煎
OYSTER OMELET

SERVES 2

INGREDIENTS

EGGS	2
FISH SAUCE	1 TEASPOON + A LITTLE TO SERVE
WHITE PEPPER	A FEW PINCHES
TAPIOCA FLOUR (STARCH)	2 TEASPOONS
CORNSTARCH	2 TEASPOONS
WATER	⅓ CUP (80 ML)
VEGETABLE OIL	1 TABLESPOON
FRESH OYSTERS, SHUCKED	8 TO 10
CILANTRO	A FEW SPRIGS
CHILE SAUCE (OPTIONAL)	TO SERVE

❶ Break the eggs into a bowl, add 1 teaspoon of fish sauce and a pinch of white pepper, then whisk well. ● In another bowl, mix the tapioca flour, cornstarch, and water.

❷ Place the oil in a frying pan over medium–high heat, ensuring it covers the whole surface. ● Pour in the tapioca and cornstarch mixture so that it covers the pan completely. ● Cook until the edges start to come away and a crispy layer is created.

❸ Add the egg mixture. ● When the mixture begins to set, break the omelet into large pieces using a wooden spatula, then stir to cook any parts that are still raw.

❹ When the omelet becomes slightly golden, add the oysters. ● Stir for 30 to 60 seconds, then add the cilantro. ● Serve with white pepper and fish sauce (or chile sauce).

包子家族

72

小吃

炸藕片
LOTUS ROOT CHIPS

SERVES 4

INGREDIENTS

FRESH LOTUS ROOTS ....**2 TO 3**
GROUND RED SICHUAN PEPPER ....⅓ **TEASPOON**

GARLIC POWDER ....⅓ **TEASPOON**
SALT ....⅓ **TEASPOON**
OIL FOR FRYING

包子家族

❶ Peel the lotus roots. ● Using a mandolin, finely slice the lotus roots and place them in cold water as you work. ● Transfer to a colander and rinse under cold running water to remove excess starch.

❷ Pat dry using paper towels. ● In a pot, heat a 2½ inch (6 cm) depth of oil to 325°F (160°C). ● Gently place 15 to 20 slices at a time into the hot oil, using tongs to separate the slices. ● Once the chips are nice and golden, remove and transfer to paper towels to drain excess oil.

❸ Combine the Sichuan red pepper, garlic powder, and salt and sprinkle this over the chips.

小吃

粽子
ZONGZI

MAKES 12 PARCELS

INGREDIENTS

PORK BELLY	1 LB 2 OZ (500 G)
CHINESE FIVE SPICE	1 TEASPOON
GLUTINOUS RICE	3 CUPS (600 G)
MUNG BEANS	14 OZ (400 G)
SALT	2 TEASPOONS
VEGETABLE OIL	A DRIZZLE
DRIED SHRIMP	1¾ OZ (50 G)
SHAOXING WINE	1 TABLESPOON
SALTED DUCK EGG YOLKS	12
COOKED CHESTNUTS (OPTIONAL)	12

ASSEMBLY

BAMBOO LEAVES	24
TWINE	12 PIECES
SOY SAUCE (OPTIONAL)	TO SERVE

❶ Cut the pork belly into 12 pieces, sprinkle on all sides with the Chinese five spice, and allow to rest overnight in the refrigerator.

❷ Soak the glutinous rice and mung beans in separate bowls of water for at least 8 hours (or overnight). ● Drain, then season with the salt and a drizzle of oil.

❸ Rinse the dried shrimp and place them in the Shaoxing wine to rehydrate. ● Soak the bamboo leaves and twine in water.

❹ To assemble, form a cone with a bamboo leaf and add the ingredients in the following order: 1 teaspoon rice, 1 tablespoon mung beans, 1 piece pork, 1 egg yolk, 1 teaspoon dried shrimp, 1 chestnut (if using), and cover with 1 teaspoon rice. ● Using another bamboo leaf, cover the exposed side of the zongzi, then fold it over the other parts of the cone form a triangular parcel. ● Secure with twine so that it does not unfold.

❺ Place the zongzi in a large pot with enough water to immerse them. Cover the surface with parchment paper or a tea towel so that everything is well submerged, then put the lid on. ● Bring to a boil and allow to simmer for 30 minutes, then turn off the heat and leave to cook, covered, for another 30 minutes. ● Then repeat these steps: cook for 30 minutes, then leave to stand, covered, for another 30 minutes.

❻ To serve, unwrap the parcels, then eat with chopsticks, holding the zongzi in your hands or on a plate. You can dip them in a little soy sauce while eating. (Sweet versions are dipped in confectioners' sugar.)

包子家族

凉拌手撕鸡
SPICY CHICKEN SALAD

SERVES 2

INGREDIENTS
CHICKEN BREAST...1 TO 2
GINGER..3 SLICES
RED ASIAN SHALLOT, CHOPPED 1

SALAD
ENGLISH CUCUMBER... ½
CELERY...1 STICK
SCALLIONS..2
CILANTRO..½ BUNCH
LETTUCE ....1 HEAD

DRESSING
LIGHT SOY SAUCE.................................1 TABLESPOON
RICE VINEGAR......................................1 TABLESPOON
SESAME PASTE (ZHI MA JIANG).............2 TABLESPOONS
SESAME OIL...1 TEASPOON
CHILE OIL..1 TABLESPOON
                                    + A LITTLE TO SERVE
WHITE SUGAR ....1 TABLESPOON

GARNISH
SESAME SEEDS

❶ Allow the chicken breast to come to room temperature. ⬤ Place 6⅓ cups (1.5 liters) water in a large pot with the ginger and shallot, then bring to a boil and add the chicken. ⬤ Boil over medium heat for 8 minutes then cover, turn off the heat, and leave to cook in the residual heat for about 15 minutes, until the chicken is fully cooked. ⬤ Drain the chicken and allow to cool completely.

❷ Cut the cooled chicken into strips.

❸ Cut the cucumber, celery, and scallions into thin matchsticks. ⬤ Remove the leaves from the cilantro stems. ⬤ Wash the lettuce and separate the leaves.

❹ Combine all the dressing ingredients in a small bowl. ⬤ Place the chicken and salad ingredients in a serving bowl, add the dressing, and mix together. ⬤ Serve with a drizzle of chile oil and a sprinkle of sesame seeds.

小吃

凉拌猪皮
PORK RIND SALAD

CHINESE CUISINE EMPHASIZES USING THE ENTIRE ANIMAL OR INGREDIENT,
REDUCING WASTE AND EMBRACING THE DIFFERENT TEXTURES. THIS RECIPE IS OFTEN MADE
AS THE STAFF MEAL WHEN PORK RIND IS LEFT FROM THE MISE EN PLACE,
BUT THE DRESSING ALSO GOES WELL WITH PIGS' EARS OR EVEN COLD NOODLES.

SERVES 2

INGREDIENTS

PORK RIND	10½ OZ (300 G)
FINELY CHOPPED GINGER	¼ CUP (30 G)
THINLY SLICED GARLIC	2 TABLESPOONS
SHAOXING WINE	2 TABLESPOONS
SOY SAUCE	2 TABLESPOONS

BLACK VINEGAR	4 TEASPOONS
DRIED CHILE	1 TEASPOON
CHOPPED SCALLION	1 STEM
SHAOXING WINE	2 TABLESPOONS
SESAME OIL	4 TEASPOONS
SALT	½ TEASPOON

DRESSING

MINCED GINGER	2 TABLESPOONS
MINCED GARLIC	1 TEASPOON
SPICY FERMENTED BEAN SAUCE (DOU BAN JIANG)	1 TEASPOON
WHITE SUGAR	½ TABLESPOON

DRESSING

YOUR CHOICE OF SCALLIONS, CILANTRO, MINT, THAI BASIL, OR OTHER FRESH HERBS

❶ Place the pork rind in a pot with cold water, cover, and bring to a boil. ● Discard the water. ● Fill the pot with water again and add the ginger, garlic, Shaoxing wine, and soy sauce. ● Bring to a boil and simmer for 1 hour. ● Remove the rind from the cooking liquid and allow to cool completely, then slice into strips.

❷ Mix all the dressing ingredients with the pork strips and serve with finely chopped scallions or fresh herbs.

包子家族

小
吃

皮蛋豆腐
TOFU AND CENTURY EGG

SERVES 2

INGREDIENTS

CENTURY EGG	1
SILKEN TOFU	9 OZ (250 G)
STORE-BOUGHT CRISPY FRIED SHALLOTS	1 TABLESPOON

WHITE SUGAR	3 TEASPOONS
FRESH RED CHILE, CHOPPED	½ (TO YOUR TASTE)

SAUCE

CILANTRO	8 SPRIGS
LIGHT SOY SAUCE	⅓ CUP (90 ML)
BLACK VINEGAR	1¼ TABLESPOONS
SESAME OIL	1¼ TABLESPOONS

TO SERVE

DRIED SHREDDED PORK	1 SMALL HANDFUL
CHOPPED SCALLION	1 TABLESPOON
FRESH RED CHILE, CHOPPED	½ (TO YOUR TASTE)

❶ Finely chop the cilantro stems (set aside 4 or 5 leaves and 1 teaspoon of sliced stems to garnish). ● Mix all the sauce ingredients in a jar and shake vigorously. ● Set aside for at least 1 hour.

❷ Peel the egg and cut it into eighths. ● Drain the tofu and carefully place it on a serving plate. ● Sprinkle the fried shallots on the tofu (reserving a little to garnish), to add texture for the egg pieces to stick to. ● Place a few egg pieces on top and arrange the rest around the tofu.

❸ Shake the sauce again, then pour it over the egg pieces and tofu. ● Garnish with the remaining fried shallots and the dried pork, scallion, chopped fresh chile, and the reserved cilantro leaves and stems.

包
子
家
族

包子和点心

BAO &
DIM SUM
83

包子和点心

包子和点心的来源
HISTORY OF BAO AND DIM SUM

包子家族

In Mandarin, dim sum is called 點心 *dian xin*, and means "touch the heart." In Cantonese, going out to eat dim sum is called *yum cha,* which means "drink tea." These translations perfectly illustrate the essence of this practice, which consists of eating small dishes served with tea. They are small because they are intended to touch the heart, rather than fill a stomach. Dim sum, as we know them today, are from Canton and began to emerge during the Silk Road era, when travelers would stop in tea houses to relax, drink tea, and sometimes eat.

Bao is a dish that is very close to our hearts. It is both simple to eat and to transport, but is also complex to make, requiring a certain expertise. In China, bao can be eaten anywhere, at any time of the day. Importantly, there is a distinction between bao and baozi. Baozi are steamed buns with filling, and can be considered a type of bao, but bao is not necessarily a baozi. Xiao long bao, for example, are small steamed bites with a thin pastry that contains a filling and a broth. They are not considered to be baozi.

包子和点心

包子分解步驟

STEP-BY-STEP BAOZI

DOUGH FOR 18 TO 20 BAOZI

STRONG BREAD FLOUR (T65)	**4 CUPS (500 G)**
BAKING POWDER	**1 TEASPOON**
SALT	**1 TEASPOON**
WHITE SUGAR	**6 TABLESPOONS**
ACTIVE DRY YEAST	**⅛ OZ (5 G)**
WARM WATER	**1 CUP (250 ML)**

❶ PREPARING THE DOUGH BY HAND

Put all the dry ingredients, except the yeast, into a large bowl. ● In a small bowl, combine the yeast and warm water, mix, and set aside until frothy. ● Pour the water-yeast mixture onto the dry ingredients. ● Using a pair of chopsticks, gently mix in circular movements from the center outwards, slowly combining the ingredients until they are no longer wet to the touch and they come together in a large ball of dough, not smooth but that holds together. ● Remove excess dough from the chopsticks and add it to the mixture. ● Place the dough on a flat, clean surface. ● Use the palms of your hands to knead the dough, incorporating the remaining flour left in the bowl. ● If the ball is sticky after 1 minute of kneading, sprinkle lightly with flour. ● If the dough is too dry, wet your hands and continue kneading until the dough is more pliable. ● Continue to knead the dough for 8 to 10 minutes, until the surface is smooth and the dough is elastic (when you push a finger into the dough, it should spring back to its original shape).

包子家族

包子和点心

❶ PREPARING THE DOUGH WITH AN ELECTRIC MIXER

Put all the ingredients into the bowl of a stand mixer fitted with the dough hook attachment. ● Mix at a low speed for 10 minutes. ● Check the elasticity of the dough as well as its texture—it should be smooth. ● Continue mixing for another 1 to 2 minutes if necessary.

❷ LET THE DOUGH RISE

Place the dough in a large clean bowl and cover with plastic wrap or a slightly damp clean tea towel. ● Leave the dough to rest in a warm place until it doubles in volume. ● The time may vary depending on the conditions in your kitchen. ● At 95°F (35°C) with some humidity, it can take as little as 15 minutes; at 70°F (21°C) with dry air, it can take much longer. ● Use the dough's size as a guide, rather than the time.

❸ KNOCK DOWN THE DOUGH

Take the dough out of its bowl and place it on a lightly floured surface. ● Knead the dough, taking care to remove large air pockets. ● As you knead, you may find that it becomes easier as the air bubbles become smaller and evenly distributed throughout the dough. ● If you cut the dough and see a lot of bubbles, continue kneading until they are barely visible.

❹ PORTION THE DOUGH

Cut the dough in half and roll into logs roughly the circumference of an apricot. Using a cookie cutter or a straight-edge knife, cut the dough into 1¾ oz (50 g) pieces. ● Lightly sprinkle the dough pieces with flour and move them around so that they are lightly coated with flour. ● Use only enough flour so that the pieces do not stick to each other or to the work surface, as using too much flour will make the dough less shiny once steamed. ● Take each piece of dough and flatten it with the base of your hand, with the less attractive side facing up.

Continued >

包子家族

包子和点心

包子分解步驟
STEP-BY-STEP BAOZI

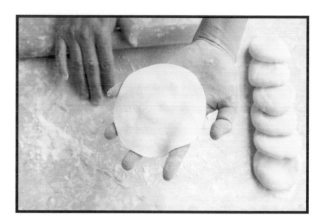

❺ ROLL OUT ROUNDS

Place a wooden rolling pin under the palm of your dominant hand. ● Start from the bottom of the dough circle and roll upwards with medium pressure, almost to the center of the dough, then roll back toward yourself. ● Using your other hand, rotate the dough 30 degrees and repeat. ● Keep turning and rolling until you have rolled the entire round. ● The center of the dough should be slightly raised—the thickness helps prevent the baozi from overflowing and balances the amount of dough around the filling. ● The edges of the dough should be thinner so that the dough is not too thick at the top after folding the baozi. ● You can roll a second time to even out the shape and thickness. ● In general, if the filling is runnier or separates easily, the circle should be larger.

❻ ADD THE FILLING AND ASSEMBLE

Place a round of dough in the palm of your hand. ● Using a spoon, add 1¼ to 1½ oz (35 to 40 g) filling to the center of the dough and make a hollow with your hand so that the dough and filling are well-supported. ● With the index finger and thumb of your other hand pointing downwards, make a "pinch" shape (picture 3). ● Make another fold along the edge of the dough and pinch gently. ● Repeat the process, rotating in the same direction (picture 4). ● You have to pinch each time with one hand, and slowly turn the base of the dough with your other hand. ● You can use the thumb of the hand holding the baozi to push the filling in if needed.

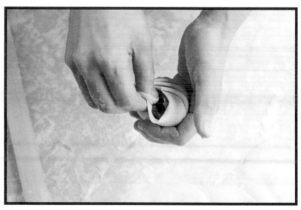

包子家族

● Continue until you can see less and less of the filling and the baozi is completely sealed. ● If you need to, pinch the top several times to ensure it is fully sealed and to prevent the baozi from exploding during cooking. ● Place each baozi in a steamer basket on squares of parchment paper or on a baking sheet lined with parchment paper, leaving at least 1¼ inches (3 cm) between them to allow them to expand.

❼ LET THE BAOZI RISE

Baozi dough will have to rise once more before cooking. ● As with the initial rising, the time it takes will depend on the temperature and humidity of the room.

Where and how to let it rise? Place them in a steam oven with 100% humidity set to 99°F (37°C) for 5 minutes. ● Or on parchment paper in a covered steamer basket set over hot water (with heat off) for 10 to 15 minutes. ● Or in a standard oven preheated to the lowest temperature, then turned off with the door ajar. After 5 minutes, the air inside the oven should be warm when you put your hand in. Place the baozi inside and leave them to rest for 5 minutes with the oven door still ajar. ● The result needs to be a dough that is less dense than after assembling the baozi, and that is soft to touch. In terms of size, they should become slightly larger.

Errors to avoid during this step:
● Allowing the dough to rise in a drafty place. This will cause the surface to dry out and crack as the dough rises. ● Allowing too much rising time, and therefore too much fermentation. This will cause the baozi to lose its shape and even open once it is cooked.

❽ STEAMING

If you choose to steam in bamboo baskets, carefully arrange the baozi on perforated parchment paper in your steamer basket before turning on the heat to avoid burning yourself with the steam. ● If you are steaming in an oven, set the oven to 200°F (100°C) (at full humidity if you have a steam oven). ● Steam for 12 minutes for baozi with a pre-cooked filling and 15 minutes if the filling is raw. ● Turn off the heat and allow to stand for 2 minutes before opening the lid of the steamer basket or the oven door. ● Bon appetit!

包子和
点心

包子
家族

蔬菜包子
VEGETARIAN BAOZI

包子和点心

MAKES 18 TO 20 BAOZI

INGREDIENTS

BAOZI DOUGH (PAGE 86)	1 RECIPE
STAR ANISE	1
CINNAMON STICK	1
VEGETABLE OIL	⅓ CUP (80 ML)
GROUND RED SICHUAN PEPPER	1 TEASPOON
DRIED BLACK MUSHROOMS	3½ OZ (100 G)
SWEET POTATO VERMICELLI	3½ OZ (100 G)

GREEN CABBAGE	10½ OZ (300 G)
CARROTS	7 OZ (200 G)
CHOPPED SCALLIONS	2 STEMS
CHOPPED GARLIC	1 TABLESPOON
CHOPPED GINGER	1 TABLESPOON
OYSTER SAUCE (SEE TIP)	2 TABLESPOONS
SALT	

❶ In a small saucepan, combine the star anise, cinnamon, oil, and Sichuan pepper and then heat gently until fragrant. ● The aim is not to fry but to infuse the oil with the flavor of the spices and bring out the fragrances.

❷ Soak the black mushrooms and vermicelli in water for 20 minutes, then drain and chop finely. ● Chop the cabbage and carrots, add salt to draw out excess water from the vegetables, and allow to stand for about 30 minutes. ● Squeeze the water from the vegetables and place them in a bowl. ● Add the black mushrooms, vermicelli, chopped scallion, garlic, and ginger, then mix. ● Add the infused oil (discarding the spices) and the oyster sauce. ● Mix again.

❸ Assemble and steam according to the step-by-step instructions on pages 86–89. ● Each baozi should contain 1¾ oz (50 g) dough and 1½ oz (40 g) filling. ● Let the baozi rise for the second time in a warm, humid place for 20 minutes. ● Steam for 14 minutes and serve immediately.

TIP

You can use vegetarian mushroom-based "oyster" sauce, or simply use regular oyster sauce if you prefer.

包子家族

包
子
和
点
心

猪肉包子
PORK BAOZI

MAKES 18 TO 20 BAOZI

INGREDIENTS

BAOZI DOUGH (PAGE 86) .... 1 RECIPE
GROUND PORK .... 1 LB 2 OZ (500 G)
COOLED PORK BROTH .... SCANT 1 CUP (200 ML)
GINGER .... 1 INCH (10 G) PIECE
LIGHT SOY SAUCE .... 2 TEASPOONS

DARK SOY SAUCE .... 2 TEASPOONS
SESAME OIL .... 1 TABLESPOON
VEGETABLE OIL .... 1 TABLESPOON
SALT .... 2 TEASPOONS
CHOPPED SCALLIONS .... ⅓ CUP (40 G)

❶ Mix the ground pork and cool broth together in a bowl until they are well combined. ● Peel and chop the ginger. ● Add the remaining ingredients except the scallions. ● Once the mixture is well combined, add the chopped scallions.

❷ Assemble according to the step-by-step instructions on pages 86–89. ● Each baozi should contain 1¾ oz (50 g) dough and 1½ oz (40 g) filling. ● Let the baozi rise for the second time in a warm, humid place for 20 minutes. ● Steam for 14 minutes and serve immediately.

包
子
家
族

包子和点心

叉烧包
CHARSIU BAO

MAKES 18 TO 20 BAO

INGREDIENTS

BAOZI DOUGH (PAGE 86)	1 RECIPE
MINCED GARLIC	2 TABLESPOONS
SLICED GINGER	2 TABLESPOONS
COARSELY CHOPPED SCALLIONS	⅓ CUP (30 G)
SHAOXING WINE	2 TABLESPOONS
SOY SAUCE	SCANT 1 CUP (200 ML)
HOISIN SAUCE	⅔ CUP (150 ML)
RED FERMENTED BEAN CURD	3½ OZ (100 G)
WHITE SUGAR	½ CUP (100 G)
WHITE PEPPER	2 PINCHES
PORK SHANK	1 LB (450 G)
HONEY	¼ CUP (100 G)
CORNSTARCH	¼ CUP (30 G)
WATER	¼ CUP (60 ML)

❶ Prepare the marinade: In a large bowl, mix the garlic, ginger, scallions, Shaoxing wine, soy sauce, hoisin sauce, fermented bean curd, sugar, and white pepper in a bowl. ● Cut the pork into two large pieces, add it to the bowl, and leave to marinate for a minimum of 3 hours, or ideally overnight.

❷ Preheat the oven to 400°F (200°C). ● Drain the pork, reserving the marinade, then roast the pork on a rack for 15 minutes until caramelized. ● Remove from the oven and brush with the honey. ● Return to the oven for 15 to 20 minutes until the pork is slightly charred on the edges. ● Remove from the oven, leave to rest, then cut the pork into approximatley ½ inch (1 cm) pieces.

❸ Pour the marinade into a pot, bring to a boil, then simmer for 20 minutes. ● Strain the liquid, then return to a simmer. ● Mix the cornstarch and water in a bowl, then pour the mixture into the hot marinade. ● Bring to a boil, stirring until the sauce thickens. ● Add the pork cubes and leave to cool.

❹ Assemble according to the step-by-step instructions on pages 86–89. ● Each bao should contain 1¾ oz (50 g) dough and 1½ oz (40 g) filling. ● Let the bao rise for the second time in a warm, humid place for 20 minutes. ● Steam for 12 minutes and serve immediately.

包子家族

包子和点心

生煎包
SHENG JIAN BAO

MAKES AROUND 15 BAO

PORK RIND JELLY

RAW PORK RIND	1 LB 2 OZ (500 G)
BOILING WATER	12⅓ CUPS (3 LITERS)
CHOPPED SCALLIONS	2½ TABLESPOONS
SLICED GINGER	1½ TABLESPOONS

FILLING

CHOPPED GINGER	1 TEASPOON
CHOPPED SCALLIONS	1¼ TABLESPOONS
WARM WATER	SCANT 1 CUP (200 ML)
SALT	1 TEASPOON
WHITE SUGAR	2 TEASPOONS
GROUND PORK	5½ OZ (150 G)
DARK SOY SAUCE	1 TEASPOON
LIGHT SOY SAUCE	1 TEASPOON

DOUGH

INSTANT YEAST	⅔ TEASPOON (2 G)
BAKING POWDER	½ TEASPOON
BAKING SODA	⅛ TEASPOON
ALL-PURPOSE FLOUR	1⅓ CUPS (160 G)
WATER	⅓ CUP (80 ML)

TO COOK AND SERVE

SUNFLOWER OIL	3 TABLESPOONS
CHOPPED SCALLIONS	⅓ CUP (20 G)
TOASTED WHITE AND BLACK SESAME SEEDS	2 TABLESPOONS

包子家族

PORK RIND JELLY PREPARATION

❶ Blanch the pork rind in the boiling water for 5 minutes, then remove, setting the water aside. ❷ Finely chop the pork rind pieces and return to the water. ● Add the chopped scallions and sliced ginger, bring to a boil, then simmer, uncovered, over medium–low heat for 2 hours. Stir occasionally so that nothing sticks to the bottom of the pot. ❸ Remove from the heat and pour through a strainer, keeping only the liquid. ❹ Pour the liquid into a container and refrigerate for 3 to 5 hours until it sets. ❺ Cut the jelly into small cubes.

FILLING PREPARATION

❶ Immerse the ginger and scallions in the warm water and set aside for 1 hour so that the water infuses with the flavors. Strain, reserving the water. ❷ Mix the salt and sugar into the ground pork, then add the soy sauces. ● Mix well, then gradually add the infused water until all the water is mixed into the filling. ❸ Knead the meat in the bowl three to four times so that the mixture is well combined. ❹ Add the jelly, ensuring the ratio of jelly to meat mixture is 1:1, and mix well. ❺ Refrigerate the filling for at least 30 minutes before you start assembling the bao.

DOUGH PREPARATION AND BAO ASSEMBLY

❶ In a large bowl, combine the yeast, baking powder, baking soda, and flour and mix together well. ❷ Gradually mix in the water. ❸ Knead the dough for 5 minutes, then cover with plastic wrap and allow to stand for 10 minutes. ● Knead again until smooth. ❹ Divide the dough into ½ to ¾ oz (15 to 20 g) portions and roll into balls. ❺ Roll out each ball into a circle about the size of your palm, then place a heaped spoonful of filling (about ¾ oz/20 g) in the center. ❻ Bring all sides to the center and fold to seal each bao according to the step-by-step instructions on pages 86–89.

COOKING THE BAO

❶ To cook the bao, heat the oil in a nonstick frying pan. ● Place the bao in the pan with the folds facing down, leaving a small space between each bao. ❷ Cook until the bottoms are golden brown, then add water until it covers ½ to ¾ inches (1 to 2 cm) of the bao (about a scant ½ cup/100 ml water). ❸ Cover the pan, then simmer until all the water has evaporated and the bao are cooked. ❹ Remove the lid, then garnish with chopped scallions and toasted sesame seeds. ● Serve hot.

生煎包
SHENG JIAN BAO
page 98

包子和点心

燒賣解步驟
WRAPPING SIU MAI

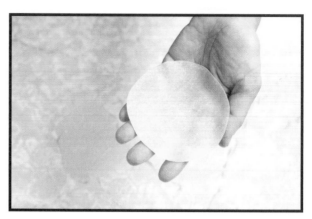

❶ Use ready-made round wonton wrappers. Prepare the filling (see recipe on page 104).

❷ Place a wonton wrapper in the the palm of your hand. Put about 1 oz (23 g) filling in the center.

❸ Bring the edges of the wrapper toward the center by gathering them up to create folds all around the filling.

包子家族

包子和点心

❹ When the wrapper is properly adhered to the filling, flatten the base of the siu mai then, using the end of a spoon, press down on the filling so that it is well packed in and as much air as possible is removed.

包子家族

包
子
和
点
心

烧卖
SIU MAI

MAKES AROUND 40 SIU MAI

INGREDIENTS
ROUND WONTON WRAPPERS **40**

FILLING
DRIED SHIITAKE MUSHROOMS .... **1¾ OZ (50 G)**
PORK SHANK .... **1 LB (450 G)**
POTATO STARCH .... **2⅔ TABLESPOONS**
SALT .... **½ TABLESPOON**

WATER .... **3½ TABLESPOONS**
PEELED SHRIMP .... **12 OZ (350 G)**
CHICKEN BOUILLON GRANULES .... **1½ TABLESPOONS**
WHITE SUGAR .... **¾ OZ (20 G)**
SESAME OIL .... **1 TEASPOON**
VEGETABLE OIL .... **1½ TABLESPOONS**
WHITE PEPPER .... **¼ TEASPOON**
SALMON ROE OR REHYDRATED GOJI BERRIES TO SERVE

❶ Prepare the filling: soak the dried shiitake mushrooms in water for 20 minutes to rehydrate them. ● Drain and chop them finely. ● Cut the pork shank into ½ inch (1 cm) cubes. ● Add the potato starch, salt, and water, then mix. ● Chop and add the shrimp and mix again. ● Lastly, add the shiitake mushrooms and remaining ingredients, mix again, and refrigerate for at least 3 hours.

❷ Place 1 oz (25 g) filling in the center of each wonton wrapper and fold as shown on pages 102–103.

❸ Arrange four siu mai in each small bamboo basket that you have (lined with parchment paper), so that they touch slightly. ● Being close together allows them to better retain their shape during cooking.

❹ Steam for 4 minutes. ● Garnish with salmon roe or rehydrated goji berries and serve immediately.

TIP
Wonton wrappers can be found in all Asian grocery stores.

包
子
家
族

包
子
和
点
心

虾饺
HAR GOW

MAKES AROUND 25 HAR GOW

INGREDIENTS
FROZEN PEELED SHRIMP ....1 LB (450 G)
POTATO STARCH ....1 TABLESPOON
LYE WATER OR SODA WATER ....1 TEASPOON
SALT ....¼ TEASPOON

FILLING
PORK FAT ....1½ OZ (40 G)
SALT ....1 TEASPOON
POTATO STARCH..2½ TEASPOONS
BAMBOO SHOOTS ....1¼ OZ (50 G)

WHITE SUGAR ....1 TABLESPOON
WHITE PEPPER ....¼ TEASPOON
CHICKEN BOUILLON GRANULES ....2¼ TEASPOONS
SESAME OIL ....½ TEASPOON

DOUGH
WHEAT STARCH ....¾ CUP (100 G)
POTATO STARCH.....................½ TABLESPOON + ½ CUP (80 G)
BOILING WATER ....SCANT 1 CUP (200 ML)
VEGETABLE OIL ....½ TABLESPOON + FOR OILING

❶ Defrost, rinse, and drain the shrimp, then chop them. ● Mix them with the potato starch until the mixture becomes sticky. ● Add the lye water or soda water and salt, then marinate for 20 to 30 minutes.

❷ Rinse the shrimp and leave them to soak in water for 45 minutes to 1 hour, changing the water regularly.

❸ Prepare the filling: cut the pork fat into small pieces, then fry until golden. ● Carefully drain and dry the shrimp, then mix in the salt and potato starch and set aside.

❹ Cut the bamboo shoots into cubes, blanch them in boiling water, then let them cool before draining well. ● Sprinkle the bamboo shoots with sugar and white pepper, add the bouillon granules and sesame oil, then add the shrimp. ● Pat and mix until the filling comes together. ● Set aside in the refrigerator.

❺ Prepare the dough: in a bowl, mix the wheat starch and the ½ tablespoon potato starch. ● Pour in the boiling water and stir quickly to form a cooked dough. ● Allow to stand for 5 minutes.

❻ Add the oil and mix. ● Add the ½ cup (80 g) potato starch and knead on your work surface until a smooth dough is formed. ● Roll the dough into a long rope about 1 inch (3 cm) in diameter, and cut it into about 25 slices, each about ½ oz (15 g).

❼ Lightly oil a wooden cutting board and place it on a flat surface, making sure it is stable (you can put a damp tea towel underneath to secure it). ● Using the blade of a Chinese cleaver, first press one piece of dough to flatten it, then press, turning it clockwise to form a semicircle. ● Repeat the same movements counter-clockwise to get a very thin circle of dough about the size of your palm. ● Repeat with the remaining pieces of dough.

❽ Place ½ oz (15 g) filling onto the center of a dough circle and fold into a parcel, pleating the edges and pinching the top to seal them. Repeat with the remaining circles and filling.

❾ Arrange closely in lined steamer baskets and steam on high heat for 3 minutes.

包
子
家
族

包子和点心

餃子分解步驟
STEP-BY-STEP JIAOZI

DOUGH FOR 15 TO 20 JIAOZI

ALL-PURPOSE FLOUR	**4 CUPS (500 G) + FOR DUSTING**
WATER	**SCANT 1 CUP (200 ML)**
SALT	**1 TEASPOON**

❶ Prepare the dough: mix the flour, water, and salt in a bowl and start kneading. ● Transfer the dough to a work surface and continue to knead until you get a smooth dough. ● Cover and leave to rest at room temperature for 1 hour.

❷ Prepare the filling (see recipe page 110).

❸ Divide the dough into four pieces to form balls, then roll them into logs of the same length and diameter.

❹ Break the log into ¾ oz (20 g) portions and roll each into a ball. ● Lightly flour each ball. ● Flatten each ball of dough with the palm of your hand. ● Use one hand to move the dough, and the other to use the rolling pin. ● Even pressure must be used over the lower part of the dough.

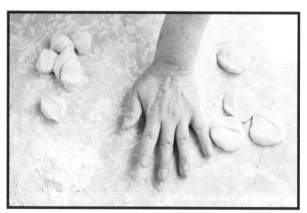

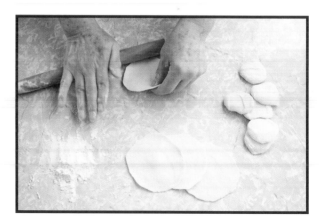

包子家族

包子和点心

❺ Rotate the dough and roll out gradually until you make a full turn. ● If the dough sticks to your work surface, put the dough round directly into the extra flour, and then continue rolling out.

❻ When the dough is about ⅛ inch (2 to 3 mm) thick, and about the size of the palm of your hand, place about 1 oz (25 g) filling in the center.

❼ Using both hands, bring your fingers inward and squeeze the top of the dumpling with your fingertips and thumbs to close it.

❽ Arrange in a steamer basket and steam or boil for 6 to 7 minutes. ● You can also cook them like guotie (see the pork and cabbage dumplings recipe, page 112): fry for 1 minute, pour in water, cover, and then remove the lid.

包子家族

包
子
和
点
心

餃子
JIAOZI

THIS RECIPE IS VERY POPULAR IN NORTHERN CHINA, WHERE YOU CAN FIND IT PREPARED WITH
MANY DIFFERENT FILLINGS AND COOKING METHODS (STEAMING, BOILING, OR PAN-FRYING).
EVEN THOUGH THE DOUGH MUST BE MADE BY HAND, THE FOLDING IS QUITE SIMPLE AND GIVES THE
JIAOZI ITS CHARACTERISTIC SHAPE, WHICH IS RECOGNIZED BY DUMPLING LOVERS AROUND THE WORLD.

MAKES 30 TO 40 JIAOZI

INGREDIENTS

JAOZI DOUGH (PAGE 108) ....2 RECIPES
GROUND PORK ....1 LB 5 OZ (600 G)
PORK BROTH...⅔ CUP (150 ML)
GARLIC CHIVES, CHOPPED ....5½ OZ (150 G)
EGG 1
OYSTER SAUCE ....1 TABLESPOON

SESAME OIL..1 TEASPOON
CHOPPED GINGER ....1 TABLESPOON
CHOPPED SCALLIONS..2 STEMS
WHITE PEPPER ....3 PINCHES
BLACK VINEGAR TO SERVE

❶ Prepare the filling: mix all the ingredients in a
bowl, then allow to rest in the refrigerator for at
least 20 minutes.

❷ Assemble and cook according to the step-by-step
instructions on pages 108–109. ● Eat with black
vinegar as a dipping sauce.

包
子
家
族

包子和点心

锅贴
PORK AND CABBAGE DUMPLINGS

MAKES AROUND 35 DUMPLINGS

INGREDIENTS
ROUND WONTON WRAPPERS 35

FILLING
CHINESE CABBAGE .... 6 TO 7 LEAVES
SALT .... 2 PINCHES + FOR SPRINKLING
GROUND PORK .... 1 LB 5 OZ (600 G)
PORK (OR CHICKEN) STOCK .... ⅔ CUP (150 ML)

LIGHT SOY SAUCE .... 1 TABLESPOON
WHITE SUGAR .... 2 PINCHES
WHITE PEPPER .... 1 PINCH
CHOPPED GINGER .... 1½ TABLESPOONS
SCALLIONS, CHOPPED .... 2 STEMS
FINELY CHOPPED SHRIMP (OPTIONAL) .... 3½ OZ (100 G)
VEGETABLE OIL FOR FRYING
BLACK VINEGAR TO SERVE

❶ Prepare the filling: cut the Chinese cabbage into thin strips lengthways, then chop finely. ● Add a little salt, mix, and set aside in a colander for 20 minutes. ● Squeeze to extract excess water.

❷ In a large bowl, mix the ground pork with the stock, soy sauce, the 2 pinches of salt, sugar, and white pepper. ● Add the chopped ginger and scallions, then mix again. ● Lastly, add the chopped cabbage to the mixture, and the chopped shrimp, if using. Mix well (to check seasoning, you can cook a small amount of filling in a frying pan).

❸ To assemble, put about 1 oz (25 g) filling in the center of each wonton wrapper and close according to the step-by-step instructions on pages 108–109.

❹ Heat a frying pan (preferably nonstick) over medium–high heat and add enough vegetable oil to cover the surface. ● Add the dumplings one at a time, nestling them together, until the pan is filled. ● Allow the underside of the dumplings to fry until lightly golden. ● Then pour in ¼ cup (60 ml) water, cover, and simmer over medium–low heat for 7 minutes. ● Remove the lid and continue to cook for 1 minute to get a crispy base. ● Transfer to a plate and serve with black vinegar.

包子家族

要抓

BAO FAMILY 包子家庭

THE
REAL WAY

人心

TO THE
HEART

BAO FAMILY 包子家庭

先抓

IS

THROUGH

BAO FAMILY 包子家庭

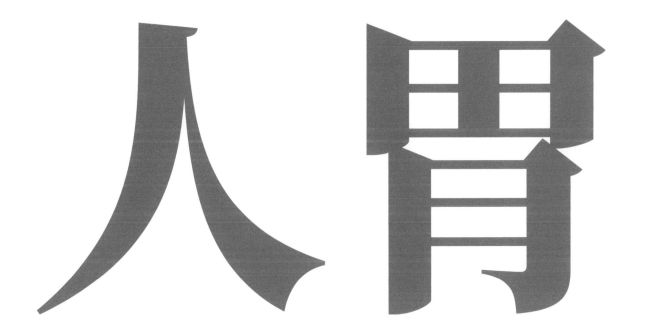

人胃

BAO FAMILY 包子家庭

THE STOMACH

包子和点心

萝卜糕
TURNIP CAKE

SERVES 2

INGREDIENTS

RICE FLOUR	¾ CUP (110 G)
WHEAT STARCH	¼ CUP (30 G)
CORNSTARCH	¼ CUP (30 G)
WATER	⅔ CUP (150 ML)
CHOPPED CHINESE SAUSAGE	2 OZ (60 G)
DRIED SHRIMP	¾ OZ (20 G)
DAIKON (WHITE RADISH)	15 OZ (420 G)
WHITE SUGAR	1 TABLESPOON
SALT	1 TEASPOON
WHITE PEPPER	½ TEASPOON
CHOPPED SCALLION	2 TABLESPOONS
SESAME CHILE OIL	1 TEASPOON
VEGETABLE OIL FOR FRYING	

❶ In a shallow bowl, mix the rice flour, wheat starch, and cornstarch with the measured water to make the breading.

❷ In a wok, heat a drizzle of vegetable oil and fry the chopped Chinese sausage and dried shrimp until cooked.

❸ Cut the daikon into thin matchsticks, then place in a saucepan with enough water to cover it, and boil until tender, 5 to 10 minutes. ● Drain the daikon, transfer to the wok with the sausage and shrimp, and mix over medium heat until combined.

❹ Add the water and cornstarch mixture to the wok with the sugar, salt, and pepper, then stir until it thickens. ● Transfer to a rectangular dish that fits in your steamer and steam for 50 minutes (or until cooked). ● Leave to cool overnight in the refrigerator.

❺ Cut the cake into 1½ to 2 inch (4 to 5 cm) squares and brown them on both sides in a nonstick frying pan with a drizzle of vegetable oil. ● Arrange the pieces of cake on two plates and garnish with chopped scallion. ● Serve with chile oil.

包子家族

包子和点心

春卷
CHINESE SPRING ROLLS

MAKES AROUND 12 ROLLS

INGREDIENTS

CHINESE CABBAGE .... 14 OZ (400 G)
SALT ....1 TEASPOON
COOKED CHICKEN BREAST .... 7 OZ (200 G)
GRATED CARROT .... 1¾ OZ (50 G)
SESAME OIL ....2 TEASPOONS

LIGHT SOY SAUCE ....2 TEASPOONS
WHITE SUGAR ....1 TEASPOON
WORCESTERSHIRE SAUCE ....TO YOUR TASTE + FOR SERVING
LARGE RECTANGULAR SPRING ROLL PASTRY SHEETS...........12
VEGETABLE OIL FOR FRYING

❶ Cut the Chinese cabbage into thin strips lengthways, then chop finely. ● Add salt, mix, and set aside in a colander for 20 minutes. ● Squeeze to extract excess water. ● Finely chop the chicken. ● Mix the chicken, cabbage, and remaining ingredients, except for the pastry, together.

❷ During assembly, cover the rolls and pastry sheets with a damp tea towel to prevent the pastry from drying out. ● To fold, place the pastry sheets on your work surface so that a corner is facing toward you. ● Put 1½ oz (40 g) of the filling in a line in the center of the pastry sheet. ● Start folding the pastry over the filling from the corner closest to you, rolling it into a cigar shape. ● Halfway through, fold the sides into the middle, then continue rolling into a cigar. ● Seal with a little water.

❸ In a large pot, heat a 2¾ inch (7 cm) depth of oil until it is 325°F (160°C). Fry the spring rolls in batches until evenly golden. ● Transfer to a plate lined with paper towels. ● Serve with Worcestershire sauce.

包子家族

包子和点心

豆豉蒸排骨
STEAMED PORK RIBS WITH GARLIC AND BLACK BEANS

SERVES 10

INGREDIENTS

BONE-IN PORK RIBS	10½ OZ (300 G)
FERMENTED BLACK BEANS (DOUCHI)	1 TABLESPOON
GARLIC	3 CLOVES
CORNSTARCH	1 TABLESPOON
LIGHT SOY SAUCE	1 TABLESPOON
SHAOXING WINE	½ TABLESPOON
VEGETABLE OIL	1 TEASPOON
SESAME OIL	½ TEASPOON
WHITE SUGAR	1 TEASPOON
SALT	½ TEASPOON
WHITE PEPPER	¼ TEASPOON

GARNISH

RED CHILE, DESEEDED AND SLICED	½
SCALLION, SLICED	1 STEM

❶ Cut the pork ribs into pieces (you can ask your butcher to do this). ● Soak in cold water for 30 minutes. ● Drain and place in a bowl.

❷ Rinse the fermented black beans with warm water to remove excess color. Drain. ● Peel and chop the garlic.

❸ Coat the ribs with the cornstarch, then add the remaining ingredients.

❹ Leave to marinate for at least 1 hour.

❺ Place the ribs and marinade in a shallow heatproof dish that fits into your steamer. ● Arrange the ribs flat in a single layer. ● Steam for 13 minutes, until cooked.

❻ Garnish with slices of red chile and scallion.

包子家族

包子和点心

马来糕
STEAMED SPONGE CAKE
MA LAI GAO

A STEAMED CAKE MADE WITH BROWN SUGAR THAT IS EATEN ALONGSIDE DIM SUM.

SERVES ABOUT 4

INGREDIENTS

MILK	¼ CUP (60 ML)
DARK BROWN SUGAR	SCANT 1 CUP (180 G)
EGGS	3
INSTANT YEAST	1 TEASPOON (3 G)
ALL-PURPOSE FLOUR	1½ CUPS (180 G)

PASTRY CREAM POWDER, CUSTARD POWDER, OR VANILLA PUDDING MIX	2⅔ TABLESPOON (20 G)
BAKING SODA	½ TEASPOON
BAKING POWDER	1 TEASPOON
SALT	½ TEASPOON
VEGETABLE OIL	¼ CUP (60 ML)

❶ In a mixing bowl, combine the milk, sugar, eggs, and yeast. ⬤ Sift in the flour and pastry cream powder, then stir to combine. ⬤ Leave the batter to rise for at least 2 hours in a warm place until air bubbles appear.

❷ Meanwhile, cover an 8 inch (20 cm) diameter bamboo basket with parchment paper, making sure all the edges are covered to prevent the batter from overflowing.

❸ Once risen, transfer 3 tablespoons of the batter to a small bowl and mix it with the baking soda, baking powder, salt, and oil until a smooth mixture is formed. ⬤ Combine this mixture with the rest of the batter, mixing well.

❹ Pour the batter into the bamboo basket and steam for 40 minutes without lifting the lid.

包子家族

汤和面条

SOUPS &
NOODLES
127

汤
和
面
条

馄饨汤
WONTON SOUP

SERVES 4

INGREDIENTS

CHICKEN CARCASS WITH SKIN AND SOME MEAT
(OR CHICKEN WINGS, SEE TIP) .... 2 LB 4 OZ (1 KG)
WATER .... 10½ CUPS (2.5 LITERS)
GINGER, CUT INTO STICKS .... 2¾ OZ (80 G)
SCALLIONS, CUT INTO STICKS .... 3 STEMS
WHITE PEPPER .... 3 PINCHES
SESAME OIL .... 1 TABLESPOON

SALT .... TO TASTE
EGG 1
CORNSTARCH + WATER MIXTURE
(1:3 CORNSTARCH TO WATER RATIO) .... 1 TEASPOON
WONTONS (SEE PAGES 168–170) 20
SPINACH .... 7 OZ (200 G)
MINT LEAVES AND SLICED SCALLIONS TO SERVE

❶ Place the chicken into a Dutch oven or large heavy pot and cover with cold water. ● Bring to a boil, then discard the water to get rid of impurities. ● Fill the pot with the measured water and add the ginger and scallions. ● Bring to a boil, then simmer over medium–low heat for 45 minutes. ● Strain the broth and add the white pepper, sesame oil, and salt, to taste.

❷ In a small bowl, combine the egg and cornstarch mixture and beat vigorously. ● Set a wok or nonstick frying pan over medium–high heat and pour in the egg mixture to create a thin layer that covers the entire surface. ● Once the edges begin to come away from the pan, lower the heat and turn the omelet over until cooked. ● Slice the omelet into thin strips.

❸ Add the wontons to the broth and cook until they float, then add the spinach and cook for another minute. ● Serve with the egg strips, mint leaves, and sliced scallions.

TIP

To obtain a rich and tasty broth, it is best to use the bones, skin, and meat of the chicken. If you use chicken wings, cut them in half to expose the meat and bone.

包
子
家
族

汤和面条

台湾红烧牛肉面
TAIWANESE BEEF NOODLE SOUP

THIS RECIPE IS QUITE DETAILED—IT TYPICALLY TAKES A WHOLE DAY OR EVEN OVERNIGHT TO MAKE. EACH ROUND OF INGREDIENTS ADDED TO THE POT SHOULD FILL YOUR HOME WITH TANTALIZING AROMAS, WHICH WILL RESULT IN MELT-IN-THE-MOUTH BEEF AND SLURPS OF SATISFACTION. IT IS AN ADVENTURE FOR THE SENSES THAT CULMINATES IN A SOUP THAT HAS BECOME A CELEBRATED DISH IN TAIWAN AND IS MADE IN THOUSANDS OF DIFFERENT WAYS ACROSS THE WORLD.

SERVES 6

INGREDIENTS

BEEF SHORT RIBS, CUT INTO PIECES .... 3 LB 5 OZ (1.5 KG)
BEEF FLANK .... 1 LB 2 OZ (500 G)
WHITE ONION, SLICED 1
GRATED GINGER .... 3 TABLESPOONS
GARLIC, CRUSHED .... 5 CLOVES
SCALLIONS, ROUGHLY CHOPPED .... 3 STEMS
LEEK, ROUGHLY CHOPPED 1
CELERY WITH LEAVES, SLICED .... 1 STEM
CARROT, SLICED 1
SALT

SPICE MIXTURE

GROUND SICHUAN RED PEPPER .... 1 TEASPOON
FENNEL SEEDS .... 1 TEASPOON
CINNAMON STICK 1
STAR ANISE 1
DRIED LIQUORICE ROOT 1
DRIED ORANGE PEEL .... 1 PIECE
DRIED CHILE 1
BAY LEAVES 2

SOUP

SPICY FERMENTED BEAN SAUCE
(DOU BAN JIANG) .... 1½ TABLESPOONS
SWEET FERMENTED BEAN SAUCE
(TIAN MIAN JIANG) .... 1½ TABLESPOONS
SPICY CHILE CRISP (LAO GAN MA) .... 1 TABLESPOON
SHAOXING WINE .... ⅓ CUP (80 ML)
LIGHT SOY SAUCE .... 3½ TABLESPOONS
DARK SOY SAUCE .... 3½ TABLESPOONS
ROCK SUGAR .... 1¾ OZ (50 G)
TOMATOES, QUARTERED 2
WATER .... 16 TO 20 CUPS (4 TO 5 LITERS)

GARNISH AND SERVING

FRESH WHEAT NOODLES .... 1 LB 5 OZ (600 G)
SMALL BOK CHOY 12
SCALLIONS, SLICED .... 2 STEMS
CILANTRO .... 1 BUNCH
FRESH RED CHILE, CHOPPED 2

包子家族

汤
和
面
条

❶ Sear the beef short rib pieces in a Dutch oven or large heavy pot with a 24-cup (6-liter) capacity until they are well browned on all sides. ● Remove the ribs and pour off and reserve just a small amount of the beef fat, leaving the rest in the pot. ● Place the beef flank in another pot and fill with water until covered by the equivalent of three thumb lengths of water. ● Bring the beef flank to a boil for 1 minute, then drain and set the meat aside.

❷ Heat the Dutch oven containing the beef fat over over medium–high heat. ● Add the onion, ginger, garlic, scallions, and leek. ● When they begin to soften and brown, add the sliced celery and carrot. ● Continue stirring for another 2 to 3 minutes, then add the spice mixture. ● If necessary, add a little of the reserved beef fat so that the spices release their fragrances. ● Next add the dou ban jiang, tian mian jiang, and chile crisp, then stir quickly. ● The thick sauces should only come into contact with the hot pot for a short time. ● Lower the heat to medium and add the wine and soy sauces, stirring to deglaze the pot. ● Let the mixture heat, then add the sugar, tomatoes, ribs, and flank. ● Fill the pot with the measured water, leaving a little room for it to simmer without boiling over.

❸ Bring to a boil, then cover and simmer for 2½ to 3 hours, skimming impurities and fat every 20 minutes or so, until the beef is tender. ● Turn off the heat and leave to cool for about 30 minutes. ● Using large tongs, carefully remove the beef pieces and set them aside.

● Strain the broth into a large container, squeezing the cooked vegetables to release their liquid. (You can throw away the vegetables as they have already released most of their flavor and nutrients, or you can keep them to eat with rice later for a fiber-rich meal lightly seasoned with the delicious broth!) ● Allow the broth to cool fully and then skim the fat from the surface. ● Taste, and add salt if necessary to release the broth's different layers of flavor.

❹ At this stage, you can put the beef back into the broth and store it in the refrigerator until you are ready to serve. ● The flavors will continue to develop and be even better to eat the next day.

❺ When you are ready to serve, fill another deep pot with water and add 2 to 3 generous pinches of salt. ● If you have chosen thin noodles, add more salt to the water, as the noodles will take less time to cook. ● Cook the noodles according to the package instructions. ● About 1 minute before the end of cooking, add the bok choy. ● Drain and divide the noodles and bok choy among large bowls. ● Reheat the beef soup if necessary, and pour the hot soup over the noodles, making sure that each bowl contains some of both meats. ● Garnish with sliced scallions, cilantro sprigs, and chopped chile.

包
子
家
族

台湾红烧牛肉面
TAIWANESE BEEF NOODLE SOUP
page 130

汤
和
面
条

香菇炖鸡
STEWED CHICKEN WITH SHIITAKE MUSHROOMS

SERVES 6

INGREDIENTS

DRIED SHIITAKE MUSHROOMS	1½ OZ (40 G)
WHOLE CHICKEN	1
LEEK	1½ OZ (40 G)
GINGER	¼ OZ (8 G)
GARLIC	1 TABLESPOON
VEGETABLE OIL	A DRIZZLE
WHITE SUGAR	1⅓ TABLESPOONS
SHAOXING WINE	3 TABLESPOONS
STAR ANISE	1
BAY LEAF	1
FERMENTED YELLOW SOYBEAN PASTE (HUANGDOU JIANG)	1 TABLESPOON
LIGHT SOY SAUCE	2 TABLESPOONS
DARK SOY SAUCE	2 TEASPOONS
SWEET POTATO VERMICELLI	5½ OZ (150 G)
SALT	3 TEASPOONS
CORNSTARCH + WATER MIXTURE (1:3 CORNSTARCH TO WATER RATIO)	4 TEASPOONS

❶ Soak the mushrooms for about 20 minutes to rehydrate them, then drain (you can keep the mushroom soaking water for cooking—it will add extra flavor). Rinse the mushrooms and set them aside. ● Cut the chicken into 10 pieces: thighs, drumsticks, wings, breasts, and tenders. ● Soak the chicken pieces in cold water, then pat dry. ● Cut the leek, ginger, and garlic into small cubes.

❷ Pour the oil into a Dutch oven or large heavy pot and slowly heat the sugar until caramelized. ● Before the caramel becomes too dark, add the chicken pieces, fry for 1 minute, then add the

Shaoxing wine, leek, ginger, garlic, star anise, bay leaf, and yellow soybean paste. ● Fry for 1 minute, then add the soy sauces. ● Add the soaking water from the mushrooms (or plain water) until all the ingredients are covered. ● Bring to a boil, then simmer, covered, over low heat for 25 to 35 minutes, until the chicken is cooked.

❸ Add the mushrooms, vermicelli, and salt and boil over medium heat for 12 minutes. ● Mix in the cornstarch and water mixture until thickened and serve.

包
子
家
族

汤
和
面
条

玉米排骨汤
PORK AND CORN SOUP

THIS SOUP IS INCREDIBLY EASY TO MAKE, EXTREMELY COMFORTING IN ANY SEASON,
AND CAN BE ENJOYED PLAIN OR WITH NOODLES AND FRESH HERBS.

SERVES 6

INGREDIENTS

**CUBED BONE-IN PORK SPARE RIBS (WITH TRIMMINGS),
CUT INTO PIECES** .... 1 LB 12 OZ (800 G)

EARS OF CORN 2
CARROT 1
SALT OR FISH SAUCE

❶ Place the pork in a Dutch oven or large heavy pot. ● The pieces with bone and cartilage will give the broth an even richer and deeper flavor. ● Pour water into the pot until the meat is covered, bring to a boil, then turn off the heat.

❷ Once the pork is cooked, discard the water, keeping the meat in the pot. ● Pour in fresh water to cover the meat, bring to a boil, then simmer for 1 hour.

❸ Cut the corn into ⅔–¾ inch (1.5–2 cm) thick slices, cut the carrot into ¾ inch (2 cm) batons, and add both to the pot. ● Simmer for 30 minutes or until the meat easily comes away from the bone. ● Taste and add salt (or fish sauce) to your liking. ● Serve immediately.

包
子
家
族

汤
和
面
条

番茄蛋花汤
TOMATO AND EGG SOUP

SERVES 4 TO 6

INGREDIENTS

TOMATOES	10⅓ OZ (300 G)
EGGS	3
FINELY CHOPPED GINGER	1½ TABLESPOONS
CHOPPED SCALLIONS	1¾ TABLESPOONS
WHITE SUGAR	2 TEASPOONS
WHITE VINEGAR	4 TEASPOONS
SHAOXING WINE	2 TEASPOONS

WATER	8½ CUPS (2 LITERS) + ¼ CUP (60 ML)
CORNSTARCH	2 TABLESPOONS
SESAME OIL	1 TEASPOON
SALT	1 TABLESPOON
WHITE PEPPER	2 PINCHES

GARNISH

CHOPPED CILANTRO AND/OR SCALLIONS)	5 STEMS

❶ Cut two of the tomatoes into eight pieces each and the remaining tomatoes into ½ inch (1 cm) cubes. ● Break the eggs into a bowl and whisk well.

❷ In a frying pan set over medium–high heat, fry the large tomato pieces with the ginger, scallions, sugar, and white vinegar to bring out the aromas, then pour in the wine. ● In a large pot, combine the remaining tomatoes with the 8½ cups (2 liters) of water, bring to a boil, and boil for 5 minutes.

❸ Dilute the cornstarch in the ¼ cup (60 ml) of water and gradually mix it into the soup so that it thickens.● Slowly pour in the egg mixture, stirring the soup with chopsticks. ● Season with the oil, salt, and pepper, and serve with the cilantro and/or scallions.

包
子
家
族

汤和面条

冬瓜排骨汤
WINTER MELON SOUP

SERVES 4 TO 6

INGREDIENTS

DRIED SHRIMP	2 OZ (60 G)
WINTER MELON (WAX GOURD)	1 LB 12 OZ (800 G)
SICHUAN PEPPER OIL	1 TEASPOON
CHOPPED GINGER	2½ TABLESPOONS
SESAME OIL	2 TEASPOONS
WHITE SUGAR	2 TEASPOONS
CILANTRO SPRIGS	½ OZ (15 G)
CHOPPED SCALLIONS (OPTIONAL)	1½ CUPS (100 G)
WATER	12½ CUPS (3 LITERS)
SALT	

❶ Soak the dried shrimp in cold water for 10 minutes. ● Peel and cut the winter melon into ¼ inch (5 mm) thick slices.

❷ Place all the ingredients into a Dutch oven or large heavy pot, reserving a little cilantro and scallions to garnish. ● Bring to a boil, then simmer until the melon is translucent. ● Season with salt to your taste, garnish, and serve immediately.

包子家族

汤和面条

酸辣汤
HOT-AND-SOUR SOUP

SERVES 4 TO 6

INGREDIENTS

PORK TENDERLOIN	3½ OZ (100 G)
DRIED SHIITAKE MUSHROOMS	1 OZ (30 G)
DRIED BLACK FUNGUS	⅔ OZ (20 G)
BAMBOO SHOOTS	7 OZ (200 G)
TOFU	7 OZ (200 G)
SCALLIONS	2 STEMS
GINGER	½ OZ (15 G)
VEGETABLE OIL	A DRIZZLE
GARLIC	¼ OZ (10 G)
LIGHT SOY SAUCE	4 TEASPOONS OR TO TASTE
DARK SOY SAUCE	2 TEASPOONS
WHITE SUGAR	1½ TABLESPOONS OR TO TASTE
CHINKIANG BLACK VINEGAR	3 TABLESPOONS OR TO TASTE
WHITE PEPPER	1 TEASPOON OR TO TASTE
CORNSTARCH + WATER MIXTURE (1:3 CORNSTARCH TO WATER RATIO)	3 TABLESPOONS
EGGS	2
CILANTRO	3 STEMS
OIL FOR FRYING	

MARINADE

EGG WHITE	1
CORNSTARCH	1 TABLESPOON
SHAOXING WINE	1 TABLESPOON
SALT	2 PINCHES
FRESHLY GROUND BLACK PEPPER	2 PINCHES

❶ Combine all the marinade ingredients in a large bowl. Add the pork and marinate for 20 to 30 minutes. ● Meanwhile, soak the shiitake mushrooms and black mushrooms in water for 20 minutes to rehydrate them, then drain, rinse, and cut them into thin matchsticks. ● Cut the bamboo shoots, tofu, pork, scallions, and ginger into thin matchsticks. ● Heat a little oil in a pan and sauté the pork until browned. Set aside.

❷ Pour a drizzle of oil into a deep Dutch oven or large heavy pot, then sauté the mushrooms, bamboo shoots, tofu, scallions, ginger, and garlic. ● Stir in the soy sauces, then add enough water to cover the ingredients by 1 inch (3 cm). ● Bring to a boil, then lower the heat and simmer gently for 20 minutes. ● Add the pork, sugar, vinegar, and white pepper, and taste. ● The soup should be sweet, sour, and salty. If necessary, adjust the seasoning by adding more white pepper, vinegar, or light soy sauce as needed.

❸ Stir in about two-thirds of the cornstarch and water mixture to thicken the broth. ● If it is still quite thin, stir in the remaining cornstarch mixture. ● Beat the eggs in a bowl. ● Slowly pour the eggs into the soup, stirring them with chopsticks to form long, thin strands of egg. ● Remove from the heat and serve, garnished with cilantro leaves.

包子家族

主菜

MAINS
147

番茄炒蛋
TOMATO SCRAMBLED EGGS

SERVES 2, WITH RICE

INGREDIENTS

TOMATOES	3
EGGS	3
SALT	1 PINCH
VEGETABLE OIL	2 TABLESPOONS + A FEW DROPS
WHITE SUGAR	1 TABLESPOON
WATER	3½ TABLESPOONS
CORNSTARCH + WATER MIXTURE (1:3 CORNSTARCH TO WATER RATIO)	1 TABLESPOON

GARNISH

CILANTRO, CHOPPED	2 STEMS
SCALLION, SLICED	1 STEM

❶ Cut a cross in the base of each tomato and plunge in boiling water for 30 seconds, then remove and peel the skin. ● Cut each tomato in half, then into quarters, and cut each quarter into three pieces. ● Beat the eggs in a small bowl and season with the salt.

❷ Pour 1½ tablespoons of oil in a frying pan set over medium-high heat, covering the whole surface. ● Pour in the eggs so that they cover the entire surface of the pan. ● When the bottom begins to set, turn the omelet over. ● As soon as the other side begins to set, break it into large pieces using a wooden spatula. ● Set aside on a plate.

❸ Pour ½ tablespoon of oil into the same pan and add the tomatoes, sugar, salt, and water, then bring to a boil for 1 to 2 minutes. ● Add the cornstarch and water mixture, simmer until the sauce thickens, then return the cooked eggs to the pan. ● Gently fry the eggs and tomatoes together to heat through, remove from the heat, and add a few drops of oil. ● Garnish with chopped cilantro and/or chopped scallion before serving.

主菜

核桃虾
WALNUT SHRIMP

SERVES 2

INGREDIENTS

RAW PEELED SHRIMP (TAILS ON)	1 LB 2 OZ (500 G)
RICE FLOUR	3 TABLESPOONS
CORNSTARCH	3 TABLESPOONS
CONDENSED MILK	¼ CUP (60 ML)
KEWPIE MAYONNAISE	¼ CUP (60 G)
HONEY	2 TEASPOONS
WALNUTS	1¼ CUPS (150 G)
WATER	2 TABLESPOONS
WHITE SUGAR	4 TEASPOONS
OIL FOR FRYING	
LIME SLICES TO SERVE	

❶ Slit the back of the shrimp to remove the veins. ● In a wide, shallow bowl, mix the rice flour and cornstarch. ● In a large mixing bowl, combine the condensed milk, mayonnaise, and honey to make the sauce.

❷ Heat a 2 inch (5 cm) depth of oil in a large pot until it is 325°F (160°C) and fry the walnuts for 2 to 3 minutes until golden. Remove from the oil using a slotted spoon and set aside, reserving the oil. ● In a small saucepan, bring the water, sugar, and walnuts to a boil. ● Stir until there is no more liquid in the pan, then allow to cool. ● Once cooled, the sugar should be crystallized but not sticky.

❸ Coat each shrimp with the dry ingredient mixture. Return the frying oil to 325°F (160°C) and fry the shrimp, in batches, until the outsides are golden brown. ● The frying time will depend on the size of the shrimp, but it should take 1½ to 2 minutes on average. ● Place the fried shrimp in the bowl containing the sauce and mix well until each one is coated. ● Add the nuts, stir again, and serve with lime slices.

TIP

Kewpie mayonnaise is best for this recipe but you can use any other mayonnaise if you can't find it.

包子家族

主菜

蒜蓉鱿鱼
GARLIC SQUID

SERVES 2

INGREDIENTS

SQUID	1 LB 2 OZ (500 G)
GARLIC	2 LARGE BULBS (100 G)
VEGETABLE OIL	SCANT 1 CUP (200 ML)
OYSTER SAUCE	2 TEASPOONS
FISH SAUCE	1½ TEASPOONS
SCALLIONS, CHOPPED	2 STEMS

❶ Score each squid with diagonal straight lines, leaving 1/16 inch (2 mm) between each cut. ● Do the same in the other direction to form a crisscross pattern. ● Blanch the squid in boiling water for 15 seconds.

❷ Chop the garlic and reserve 1 tablespoon. ● Fry the remaining garlic with all the oil except for a tablespoon in a frying pan over low heat. ● The garlic will start to foam slightly, releasing moisture. ● When it starts to brown, turn off the heat. ● If the garlic has become over-browned and turned black, discard it and try again. ● This step is key to achieving the correct result for this recipe—burnt garlic will result in a bitter taste.

❸ Pour the remaining oil into a wok over medium–high heat. ● Add the remaining 1 tablespoon of garlic, fry until softened, and pour in 1 tablespoon of the garlic oil (including fried garlic pieces). ● Over high heat, add the squid and stir-fry rapidly until just tender. ● Add the oyster sauce, fish sauce, and scallions and stir again until the sauce is evenly distributed. ● Serve immediately with a drizzle more garlic oil. ● Any remaining garlic oil can be reserved in a jar, well covered, for 2 weeks.

包子家族

主菜

红烧鱿鱼
HONGSHAO SQUID

SERVES 2

INGREDIENTS

GINGER, COARSELY CHOPPED .... 1 PIECE
SHAOXING WINE..2 TABLESPOONS
SCALLIONS, CHOPPED ....5 STEMS
SQUID CUT INTO PIECES ....1 LB 2 OZ (500 G)
CHOPPED GARLIC...1 TEASPOON
FINELY CHOPPED GINGER ....1 TEASPOON
VEGETABLE OIL ....A DRIZZLE + A FEW DROPS
SPICY FERMENTED BEAN SAUCE
(DOU BAN JIANG)..1 TEASPOON
RED BELL PEPPER, CHOPPED....................3½ OZ (100 G)

GREEN BELL PEPPER, CHOPPED..........................3½ OZ (100 G)
RED ASIAN SHALLOTS, CUT INTO MATCHSTICKS.................... 3
CILANTRO...3 STEMS

SAUCE

SHAOXING WINE...1 TEASPOON
LIGHT SOY SAUCE ....1 TEASPOON
DARK SOY SAUCE ....A FEW DROPS
BLACK VINEGAR ....½ TEASPOON
CORNSTARCH + WATER MIXTURE
(1:3 CORNSTARCH TO WATER RATIO).................2 TEASPOONS

❶ Bring a pot of water to a boil with the coarsely chopped ginger, Shaoxing wine, and a few scallion pieces and boil the squid for 30 seconds to remove impurities. ⬤ Drain and set aside.

❷ Prepare the sauce by mixing the Shaoxing wine, soy sauces, black vinegar, and cornstarch and water mixture.

❸ In a wok over medium–high heat, sauté the garlic and ginger in a drizzle of oil. ⬤ Then add the dou ban jiang, bell peppers, and shallots and fry for 1 minute. ⬤ Add the squid and fry for 20 seconds. ⬤ Pour in the sauce and stir for another 10 seconds (everything must happen very quickly so as not to overcook the squid).

❹ Add a few drops of oil to give the dish a glossy finish and garnish with cilantro.

包子家族

豉椒炒蜆
WOK-FRIED CLAMS

SERVES 2

INGREDIENTS

CLAMS	10½ OZ (300 G)
SHAOXING WINE	1 TABLESPOON
LIGHT SOY SAUCE	1 TABLESPOON
WHITE SUGAR	1 TEASPOON
RED ASIAN SHALLOTS	2
WHITE PARTS OF SCALLION	1 OZ (30 G)
FRESH CHILE	1
RED BELL PEPPER	3½ OZ (100 G)
VEGETABLE OIL	1 TABLESPOON
CHOPPED GARLIC	⅔ TABLESPOON
CHOPPED GINGER	⅓ TABLESPOON
SESAME OIL	A FEW DROPS
CILANTRO, CHOPPED	2 STEMS
SALT	

❶ Soak the clams in salted water for at least 2 hours, then rub the shells well to remove any impurities. ● Rinse.

❷ To make the sauce, mix the Shaoxing wine, soy sauce, and sugar in a bowl. ● Finely chop the shallots, the white part of the scallions, and fresh chile. ● Cut the bell pepper into thin matchsticks.

❸ In a wok over medium heat, heat the vegetable oil and sauté the garlic, ginger, scallion, shallots, half the chile, and the bell pepper for 30 seconds. ● Add the clams. ● When the clams start to open, add the sauce and stir until they all open.

❹ Pour a few drops of sesame oil into the wok and serve with chopped cilantro and the remaining fresh chile.

包子家族

青口贝
WOK-FRIED MUSSELS

SERVES 2

INGREDIENTS

MUSSELS .... 10½ OZ (300 G)
SCALLIONS .... 3 STEMS
GARLIC .... 1 CLOVE
SHAOXING WINE .... 1 TABLESPOON
LIGHT SOY SAUCE .... 1 TABLESPOON
WHITE VINEGAR .... ½ TABLESPOON
SPICY FERMENTED BEAN SAUCE
(DOU BAN JIANG) .... ½ TABLESPOON

WHITE SUGAR .... 1 TABLESPOON
CHOPPED GINGER .... 1 TEASPOON
CORNSTARCH + WATER MIXTURE
(1:3 CORNSTARCH TO WATER RATIO) .... 1½ TABLESPOONS
SESAME OIL .... A FEW DROPS
CILANTRO .... 1 TO 2 STEMS
OIL FOR FRYING

❶ Soak the mussels in salted water for at least 2 hours, then rub the shells well to remove any impurities. ● Rinse.

❷ Coarsely chop the white parts of the scallions into chunks and finely chop the green parts. ● Cut the garlic clove into 5 or 6 slices.

❸ To make the sauce, mix the Shaoxing wine, soy sauce, white vinegar, dou ban jiang, and sugar in a bowl until the sugar is completely dissolved.

❹ Heat a little oil in a wok over medium heat and stir-fry the garlic, ginger, and white scallion chunks for 30 seconds. ● Add the mussels. ● When they start to open, add the sauce, then stir in the cornstarch and water mixture. ● Stir until all the mussels open (discard any that do not).

❺ Pour a few drops of sesame oil into the wok and serve immediately, garnished with cilantro and scallion greens.

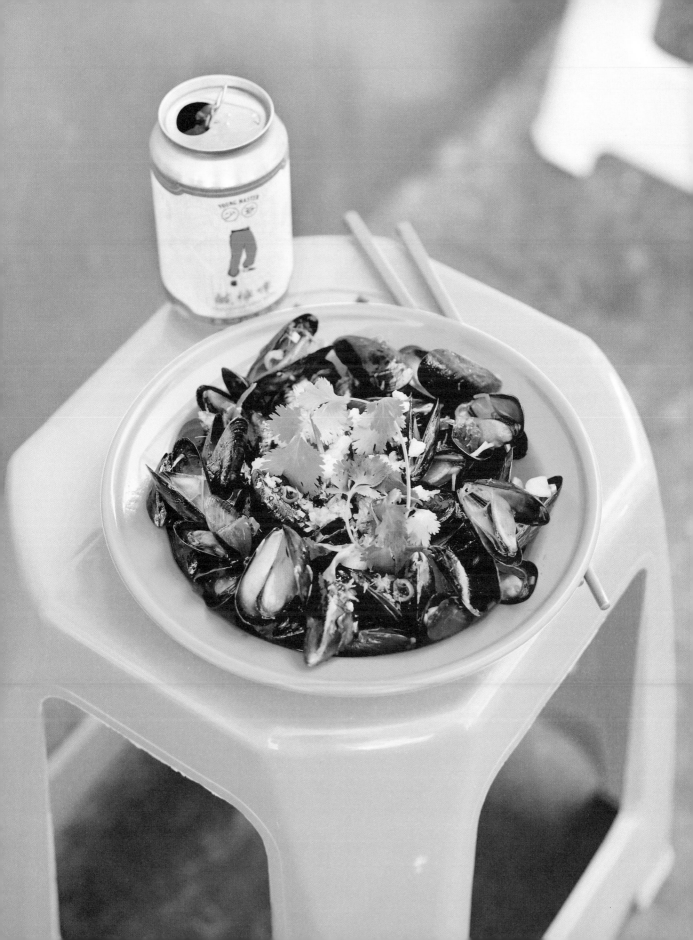

主菜

如何正确使用筷子
HOW TO USE CHINESE CHOPSTICKS CORRECTLY

① ② ③ ④

包子家族

主
菜

❶ Do not stick your chopsticks upright in your bowl! This reminds us of the incense sticks arranged near the offerings made to the deceased. Instead, place them next to or on the edge of your bowl. **❷** Do not use your chopsticks to pass food to others. **❸** Do not hit the dishes with your chopsticks because this implies begging for food and it is considered impolite. **❹** Don't cross your chopsticks over each other! Always place them side by side.

❺ Do not use your chopsticks separately, and do not stick your chopsticks in your food in order to pick it up. **❻** Do not leave your chopsticks in your mouth for a long time, or lick your chopsticks. It is very impolite and unhygienic, since you use your own chopsticks to serve yourself from shared dishes. **❼** Do not use your chopsticks to pull or bring a dish closer to yourself. **❽** Do not point at someone with your chopsticks. It is just like pointing a finger and it is considered rude.

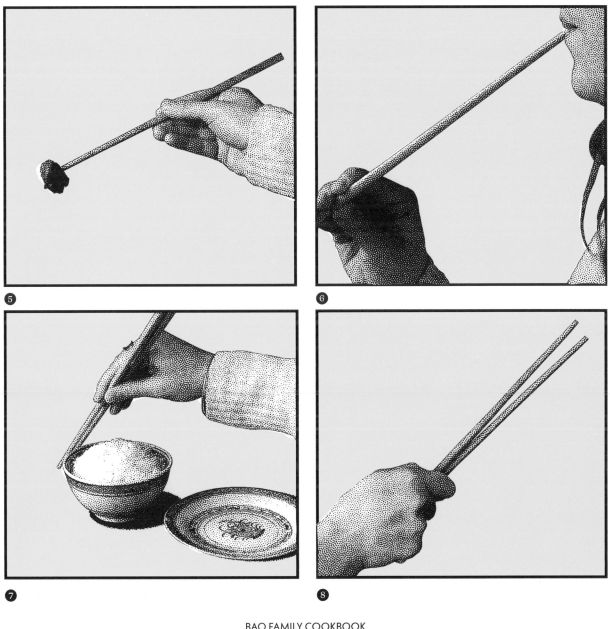

❺

❻

❼

❽

包
子
家
族

主菜

清蒸鱼
STEAMED FISH

SERVES 4

INGREDIENTS

WHOLE FISH (BASS OR SEA BREAM)	1 LB 5 OZ (600 G)
SHAOXING WINE	2 TABLESPOONS
VEGETABLE OIL	3 TABLESPOONS
GINGER	3 TO 4 SLICES
SCALLIONS	2 STEMS
SALT	

GARLIC, CRUSHED	1 CLOVE
SCALLIONS	6 STEMS
WATER	1⅔ CUPS (400 ML)
WHITE SUGAR	2 TABLESPOONS
LIGHT SOY SAUCE	1 TABLESPOON
DARK SOY SAUCE	1 TABLESPOON

SAUCE

DRIED SHIITAKE MUSHROOMS	3 TO 5
GINGER	1 PIECE
VEGETABLE OIL	A DRIZZLE

GARNISH

CARROT	½
LEEK, WHITE PART	1
GREEN BELL PEPPER	¼
VEGETABLE OIL	2 TABLESPOONS

❶ Prepare the sauce: soak the shiitake mushrooms in water for 20 minutes to rehydrate, then drain and rinse them. Peel and roughly cut the ginger into three pieces. ● Heat the oil in a large pot and fry the garlic, drained shiitake mushrooms, scallion stems, and ginger pieces for about 1 minute. ● Once the mixture is fragrant, pour in the water, sugar, and soy sauces and bring to a boil. ● Allow to simmer for about 10 minutes until the liquid reduces by half. ● Strain and set the sauce aside.

❷ Prepare the fish: make an incision in the belly and gut the fish. ● Rinse it under cold water, then pat dry with paper towels. ● Massage the whole fish with the Shaoxing wine and vegetable oil, then insert the ginger slices and scallion stems into the belly. ● Salt lightly and let stand for 5 minutes.

❸ Place in a steamer basket and steam the fish for 8 minutes (if the fish is large, cook for 10 minutes).

❹ Meanwhile, prepare the garnish—cut the carrot, leek, and pepper into thin matchsticks. ● Blanch them in boiling water for 1 minute.

❺ Heat the vegetable oil in a small saucepan over medium–high heat until slightly smoking.

❻ Once the fish is cooked, transfer it to a large serving dish and pour the sauce around the sides. ● Place the vegetables on the fish to garnish, then gently pour the warm oil onto the fish skin to add flavor to the dish.

包子家族

主菜

糖醋鱼
SWEET-AND-SOUR FISH

SERVES 4

INGREDIENTS

WHOLE FISH (BASS OR SEA BREAM) .... 1 LB 5 OZ (600 G)
EGGS, BEATEN 4
CORNSTARCH .... ⅓ CUP (50 G)
VEGETABLE OIL FOR FRYING

SAUCE

KETCHUP .... 3 TABLESPOONS
WHITE SUGAR .... 5 TABLESPOONS

RICE VINEGAR .... SCANT ½ CUP (100 ML)
DRIED CHILE FLAKES .... 1 TABLESPOON
FRESH PINEAPPLE 1
CORN KERNELS .... 2 TABLESPOONS
GREEN PEAS .... 2 TABLESPOONS
SALT .... 2 PINCHES

❶ Prepare the sauce: In a pot, heat the ketchup, sugar, rice vinegar, and chile flakes over low heat, stirring occasionally to dissolve the sugar. ● Allow to reduce. ● Meanwhile, chop the pineapple into small pieces. ● Once the sauce has reduced slightly, add the pineapple, corn, and peas. ● Season with the salt and set aside.

❷ Prepare the fish by cutting off the fins and removing the scales. ● Make an incision in the belly and gut the fish. ● Rinse it under cold water, then pat dry with paper towels. ● Cut off the head of the fish and set aside.

❸ Gently remove the backbone of the fish, making sure that the fillets remain attached to the tail. ● Using a pair of tweezers, remove the remaining bones and score (without piercing the skin) each fillet to create a crisscross pattern. ● Immerse the head and body of the fish in iced water to shrink the skin.

❹ In a wok or frying pan large enough to hold the fish, heat a 3 inch (8 cm) depth of oil to 350°F (180°C). ● While the oil is heating, dip the fish and head into the beaten eggs, then the cornstarch, making sure everything is well coated. ● Gently place the fish and head into the oil using a stainless steel skimmer to maintain the shape of the fish. ● Fry until nicely golden (6 to 8 minutes), then transfer to the serving platter.

❺ Warm the sauce over low heat and pour it over the fish.

包子家族

主菜

馄饨解
步骤
WONTON
FOLDING

❶ Make the filling (see recipes on pages 170 and 172).

❷ Place a wonton wrapper in your hand with one corner facing up.

❸ Put 1 oz (25 g) filling in the center of the dough, forming a rectangle along the length of the dough.

包子家族

主菜

❹ Using the tip of your finger, draw a line of water along the wonton wrapper, just above the filling.

❺ Take the bottom of the wrapper and place it up to the water mark, then roll the filling upwards so that the filling is almost aligned with the top of the wrapper.

❻ Lightly wet one end of the wonton, then bring the other end back over by wrapping it around your fingers. Place the wet end on the other dry end and pinch until both are sealed together.

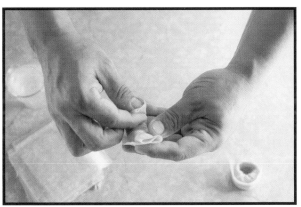

包子家族

炸鲜虾馄饨
FRIED SHRIMP WONTONS

MAKES AROUND 35 WONTONS

INGREDIENTS
RAW SHELL-ON SHRIMP.....................................2 LB 4 OZ (1 KG)
FRESH LOTUS ROOTS..1 LB 2 OZ (500 G)
CHOPPED SCALLIONS..1⅓ CUPS (100 G)
CHOPPED GINGER...1¾ TABLESPOONS
WHITE PEPPER...1 PINCH
LIGHT SOY SAUCE..¼ CUP (60 ML)

SHAOXING WINE...¼ CUP (60 ML)
SESAME OIL...2 TABLESPOONS
OIL FOR FRYING

OTHER
WONTON WRAPPERS..35
CHILE OIL

❶ Peel the shrimp and cut them into small pieces. ● Peel the lotus roots and use a food processor to pulse them into tiny pieces. ● Mix the shrimp and lotus roots with the remaining ingredients.

❷ Fill and fold the wontons according to the instructions on pages 168–169. ● Wontons can be stored in the refrigerator for a maximum of 2 hours before cooking (to avoid the wonton wrappers becoming moist from the filling, which will cause them to stick together).

❸ In a pot, heat a 3 inch (8 cm) depth of oil until it is 325°F (160°C) and fry the wontons in batches until they are nicely golden. ● Serve with chile oil.

主
菜

红油抄手
CHILE OIL WONTONS

MAKES AROUND 35 WONTONS

INGREDIENTS

RAW SHELL-ON SHRIMP......................................**2 LB 4 OZ (1 KG)**
FRESH LOTUS ROOTS...**1 LB 2 OZ (500 G)**
CHOPPED SCALLIONS..**1½ CUPS (100 G)**
CHOPPED GINGER..**1¾ TABLESPOONS**
WHITE PEPPER...**1 PINCH**
LIGHT SOY SAUCE..**¼ CUP (60 ML)**
SHAOXING WINE...**¼ CUP (60 ML)**
SESAME OIL..**2 TABLESPOONS**

OTHER

WONTON WRAPPERS..**35**
CHILE OIL
HERBS (SUCH AS SCALLIONS, CILANTRO, MINT, THAI BASIL)
SESAME SEEDS

❶ Peel the shrimp and cut them into small pieces. ● Peel the lotus roots and use a food processor to pulse them into tiny pieces. ● Mix the shrimp and lotus roots with the remaining ingredients.

❷ Fill and fold the wontons according to the instructions on pages 168–169. ● Wontons can be stored in the refrigerator for a maximum of 2 hours before cooking (to avoid the wonton wrappers becoming moist from the filling, which will cause them to stick together).

❸ Cook the wontons in a pot of boiling salted water for 5 minutes, then drain and transfer to a bowl or shallow plate. ● Pour chile oil over the top and garnish with fresh herbs and sesame seeds.

包
子
家
族

主
菜

北京烤鸭
PEKING DUCK

SERVES 4 to 6

INGREDIENTS

WHOLE DUCK (GUTTED)	1
MINCED GINGER	2 TABLESPOONS
CHOPPED RED ASIAN SHALLOTS	2
SCALLION, CHOPPED	1 STEM
CUCUMBER, SLICED INTO THIN STICKS	1
LEEK, WHITE PART, SHREDDED	1
HOISIN SAUCE	
STEAMED CHINESE BUNS OR PANCAKES	

MIXTURE FOR MASSAGING THE DUCK

HOISIN SAUCE	2 TABLESPOONS
CHINESE FIVE SPICE	2½ TEASPOONS
MINCED GINGER	2 TEASPOONS
CHOPPED GARLIC	2 TEASPOONS
SALT	1 TEASPOON

GLAZE

WATER	3½ TABLESPOONS
RICE VINEGAR	GENEROUS ½ CUP (140 ML)
RED WINE VINEGAR	5 TABLESPOONS
MALT SYRUP	2 TABLESPOONS

❶ Clean the duck and remove any remaining feathers. ● Boil a large pot of water. ● Use a hook or hold the duck by the neck above the boiling pot. ● Pour large ladlefuls of hot water onto the skin so that it begins to tighten. ● Repeat until all the duck skin is nice and tight.

❷ Make the mixture to massage the duck by combining all the ingredients. ● Rub the inside of the duck generously with the mixture, then place the ginger, shallots, and chopped scallion inside as well. ● Sew the opening closed with a large needle and kitchen twine.

❸ Heat the glaze ingredients in a saucepan until the malt syrup dissolves. ● Brush the duck evenly with the glaze. ● Hang the duck to dry (use a fan if necessary). ● Once the skin is dry to the touch, the duck can be stored in the refrigerator overnight (uncovered), so that the skin dries out even further.

❹ Preheat the oven to 400°F (200°C) and place the rack at the lowest level of the oven. ● Place the duck in the oven with the breast facing up. ● Roast for about 25 minutes, then lower the temperature to 350°F (180°C) and cook until the skin is crispy and the internal temperature reaches 175°F (80°C)—check by inserting a meat thermometer into the thickest part of the thigh. ● Remove the duck from the oven.

❺ See page 176–177 for how to slice and eat Peking duck. Slice the duck and serve immediately, with thinly sliced cucumber sticks, shredded white leek, hoisin sauce, and steamed Chinese buns or pancakes.

包
子
家
族

主菜

北京烤鸭的正确吃法
HOW TO EAT PEKING DUCK

包子家族

主菜

Peking duck is a typical dish from the city of Beijing. Originally it was a royal dish, which gradually became popular with everyone. The way the duck is cut is precise and very important. The crispy skin is cut into equal slices with a little fat and sometimes a little meat. In the traditional version of the dish, it is the skin that is especially important, and it is not necessary to serve it with meat. We start with the back or the belly then move on to the thighs, placing everything on a plate as the duck is cut. First, the skin is served with pancakes, hoisin sauce, and shredded leeks and cucumbers. The meat is used to make a main dish that is usually wok-fried (for example, fried rice with duck, or stir-fried broccoli with duck). Finally, the bones are used to make a broth to be served with the meal.

包子家族

主菜

海南鸡
HAINANESE CHICKEN RICE

SERVES 2

INGREDIENTS

SMALL WHOLE CHICKEN	1
SESAME OIL	1 TABLESPOON

BROTH

GINGER	¾ OZ (20 G)
CHOPPED GARLIC	2 CLOVES
BAY LEAVES	2
CHOPPED SCALLION	1 STEM
LEMONGRASS	1 STICK
SALT	½ TABLESPOON
WHITE SUGAR	1 TABLESPOON
WATER	10½ CUPS (2.5 LITERS)

RICE

GARLIC	1 CLOVE
RED ASIAN SHALLOT	1
VEGETABLE OIL	2 TABLESPOONS
JASMINE RICE	1⅓ CUPS (280 G)
CHICKEN BROTH	GENEROUS 2 CUPS (500 ML)

GINGER SAUCE

GRATED GINGER	2 TABLESPOONS
SALT	½ TEASPOON
CHINESE FIVE SPICE	1 SMALL PINCH
VEGETABLE OIL	3 TABLESPOONS

SWEET SOY SAUCE

LIGHT SOY SAUCE	3 TABLESPOONS
DARK SOY SAUCE	½ TABLESPOON
WHITE SUGAR	2 TABLESPOONS

CHILE SAUCE

LONG RED CHILES	2
GARLIC	1 CLOVE
WHITE SUGAR	¼ CUP (50 G)
SALT	1 PINCH
RICE VINEGAR	SCANT ½ CUP (100 ML)

GARNISH

SCALLION, SLICED	1 STEM
CILANTRO	2 STEMS
CUCUMBER, SLICED	1

❶ In a large pot, combine all the broth ingredients and heat gently for 5 minutes, then place the whole chicken into the pot and bring to a boil. ● Allow to simmer over medium heat for 10 minutes, then remove from the heat and leave covered for 20 minutes.

❷ Remove the chicken and immediately immerse it in a bowl of cold water to firm up the skin and stop it cooking further (keep the infused broth for cooking the rice).

❸ Once the chicken has cooled, drain and transfer it to a serving dish or plate and brush the skin with the sesame oil.

❹ Prepare the rice: chop the garlic and finely chop the shallot. ● Fry in a pot with the oil. ● Add the rice and stir until each grain is coated with oil. ● Pour in the chicken broth and stir gently.

● Bring to a boil, then simmer, covered, over low heat for about 15 minutes or until all the liquid has been absorbed and the rice is cooked.

❺ Prepare the ginger sauce: mix the ginger, salt, and Chinese five spice in a bowl. ● Heat the oil in a small saucepan until it starts smoking. ● Pour it gently over the ginger mixture.

❻ Prepare the soy sauce: mix all the ingredients in a bowl until the sugar has dissolved completely.

❼ Prepare the chile sauce: cut the chiles into ½ inch (1 cm) pieces. ● Blend with the other ingredients in a small food processor.

❽ Serve the chicken with the different sauces and garnish with sliced scallion and cilantro. ● Place the sliced cucumber rounds on a plate to accompany this dish.

包子家族

主菜

椒盐鸡肉
SALT-AND-PEPPER CHICKEN

SERVES 2

INGREDIENTS

CHICKEN THIGHS..............................1 LB 2 OZ (500 G)
BEATEN EGG 1
RED BELL PEPPER ....1¼ OZ (50 G)
GREEN BELL PEPPER ....1¼ OZ (50 G)
VEGETABLE OIL ....2 TABLESPOONS
CHOPPED GINGER ....1 TEASPOON
CHOPPED GARLIC................................2 TEASPOONS
DRIED CHILE FLAKES ....1 TEASPOON
FRIED GARLIC ....1 TABLESPOON

SALT...1 TEASPOON
FRESHLY GROUND BLACK PEPPER.....................½ TEASPOON
SCALLION, CHOPPED .... 1 STEM
OIL FOR FRYING

BREADING

POTATO STARCH..⅔ CUP (100 G)
ALL-PURPOSE FLOUR.....................SCANT ⅓ CUP (50 G)
GARLIC POWDER ....2 TABLESPOONS
CHINESE FIVE SPICE ....1 TABLESPOON

❶ Mix all the breading ingredients together and set aside.

❷ Cut the chicken into 1 oz (30 g) pieces, place in a large bowl with the beaten egg, and mix.

❸ Cut the bell peppers into thin matchsticks.

❹ Coat each piece of chicken with the breading and place on a dish. ● Heat a depth of 3 inches (8 cm) oil in a pot until it is 325°F (160°C) and fry a few chicken pieces at a time for 2 minutes, until the breading is golden brown and the chicken is cooked. Remove and drain on paper towels.

❺ Heat a pan over medium–high heat and pour in the vegetable oil, then add the ginger, garlic, bell peppers, and chile flakes. ● Fry until the peppers are just cooked. ● Add the fried chicken, fried garlic, salt, and freshly ground pepper. ● Garnish with the chopped scallion and serve.

包子家族

主菜

宫保鸡丁
KUNG PAO CHICKEN

SERVES 2

INGREDIENTS	
CHICKEN THIGHS	14 OZ (400 G)
SOY SAUCE	1 TABLESPOON
SHAOXING WINE	1 TABLESPOON
SALT	⅓ TEASPOON
WHITE SUGAR	1 TEASPOON
WATER	2 TABLESPOONS
CHINKIANG BLACK VINEGAR	1 TEASPOON
CHOPPED GARLIC	2 TEASPOONS
SCALLION, SLICED	2 STEMS
DRIED WHOLE CHILES, CHOPPED	2
CORNSTARCH + WATER MIXTURE (1:3 CORNSTARCH TO WATER RATIO)	1 TABLESPOON
PEANUTS	⅓ CUP (50 G)
SICHUAN PEPPER OIL	1 TEASPOON
OIL FOR FRYING	

MARINADE	
SHAOXING WINE	1 TABLESPOON
RICE WINE VINEGAR	1 TEASPOON
LIGHT SOY SAUCE	2 TEASPOONS
WHITE SUGAR	1 TEASPOON
EGG WHITE	1
CORNSTARCH	½ TEASPOON
WATER	2 TEASPOONS
SALT	1 PINCH
WHITE PEPPER	1 PINCH
VEGETABLE OIL	2 TEASPOONS

❶ Cut the chicken into approximately ½ inch (1.5 cm) pieces.

❷ Mix the marinade ingredients in a container, then add the chicken thighs and leave to marinate for at least 20 minutes.

❸ Sauté the chicken pieces in a little oil until they are just cooked.

❹ Mix the soy sauce, Shaoxing wine, salt, sugar, water, and black vinegar in a bowl.

● In a frying pan over medium–high heat, heat a little oil and brown the chopped garlic, half of the scallion, and the dried chiles. ● Add the chicken and stir for 30 seconds. ● Pour in the soy sauce mixture, mix, and then stir in the cornstarch and water mixture until each piece of chicken is coated with sauce.

❺ Add the peanuts, remaining scallion, and Sichuan pepper oil, stir one last time, and serve immediately.

包子家族

主菜

湖南回锅肉
TWICE-COOKED HUNAN PORK

SERVES 2

INGREDIENTS

PORK BELLY	1 LB 2 OZ (500 G)
GARLIC SCAPES	3½ OZ (100 G)
SCALLIONS	2 STEMS
LIGHT SOY SAUCE	3½ TABLESPOONS
SHAOXING WINE	3½ TABLESPOONS
VEGETABLE OIL	2 TABLESPOONS
SALT	1 TEASPOON
SPICY FERMENTED BEAN SAUCE (DOU BAN JIANG)	1 TEASPOON
RICE VINEGAR	2 TABLESPOONS
SWEET FERMENTED BEAN SAUCE (TIAN MIAN JIANG)	1 TEASPOON
FERMENTED BLACK BEANS (DOUCHI)	½ TABLESPOON
GROUND RED SICHUAN PEPPER	½ TABLESPOON
MINCED GARLIC	2 TEASPOONS
MINCED GINGER	1½ TABLESPOONS
CHOPPED FRESH GREEN CHILES	⅔ CUP (100 G)
WHITE SUGAR	1 TEASPOON
CILANTRO	

❶ Start by removing the rind from the pork belly (it can be used for the pork rind salad, see recipe page 78) and cook the pork belly in boiling water for 25 to 30 minutes, or until fully cooked. ● Once cooked, cool in an iced water bath, then thinly slice into ¹⁄₁₆ inch (2 mm) thick slices. ● Cut the garlic scapes and scallions into 2 inch (5 cm) chunks. ● Mix the soy sauce and the Shaoxing wine in a bowl and set aside.

❷ Heat 1 tablespoon of the vegetable oil in a large frying pan and brown the pork slices, season with the salt, then remove and set aside. ● In the same frying pan, stir-fry the dou ban jiang, rice vinegar, tian mian jiang, fermented black beans, and Sichuan pepper in the remaining oil for 30 seconds, then stir in the garlic and ginger. ● Stir-fry for 1 minute, then add the garlic scapes, green chile, and scallions. ● Stir-fry for 1 minute, then add the pork and sugar. ● Stir-fry again until everything is well coated. ● Garnish with cilantro and serve.

包子家族

主菜

红烧肉
HONGSHAO BRAISED PORK

SERVES 2

INGREDIENTS

PORK BELLY	1 LB 2 OZ (500 G)
GINGER	7 SLICES
SHAOXING WINE	2 TABLESPOONS
SCALLIONS	3 TO 5 STEMS
VEGETABLE OIL	¼ CUP (60 ML)
ROCK SUGAR	1¾ OZ (50 G)
WATER	1⅔ CUPS (400 ML) + 1 TABLESPOON
STAR ANISE	1

BAY LEAVES	3
CINNAMON STICK	½
SICHUAN PEPPER OIL (OPTIONAL)	1 TEASPOON
SALT	1 TEASPOON
WHITE PEPPER	⅓ TEASPOON
LIGHT SOY SAUCE	1 TEASPOON
DARK SOY SAUCE	½ TEASPOON
CORNSTARCH + WATER MIXTURE (1:3 CORNSTARCH TO WATER RATIO)	2 TEASPOONS

❶ Cut the pork belly into 1 inch (3 cm) cubes, then place them in a pot with 6⅓ cups (1.5 liters) of boiling water, 2 slices of the ginger, and the Shaoxing wine. ● Skim off impurities occasionally, then remove the pork from the pot. ● Finely chop the scallions, separating the whites from the greens.

❷ In a wok over medium–high heat, fry 3 slices of ginger in 1 tablespoon of the vegetable oil. ● Add the pork and fry until golden, then set aside in a bowl.

❸ In the same wok set over low to medium heat, start making the caramel with the rock sugar, 1 tablespoon of the oil, and 1 tablespoon of water. ● Stir until the mixture becomes golden, then pour in 1⅔ cups (400 ml) of hot water (the caramel should turn an amber color).

❹ In a deep pot, fry 2 slices of the ginger, the star anise, bay leaves, cinnamon, white parts of the scallions, Sichuan pepper oil (if using), and 2 tablespoons of vegetable oil, then add the pork and caramelized liquid, topping it up with water if the pork is not completely covered. ● Season with the salt and pepper and pour in the soy sauces, then simmer over low heat for at least 1½ hours.

❺ At the end of cooking, the meat should be tender and the sauce well reduced. ● Add the cornstarch and water mixture and let it thicken for 1 minute. ● Serve, garnished with the chopped scallion greens.

包子家族

主菜

狮子头
LION'S HEAD STEWED MEATBALLS

MAKES AROUND 15 MEATBALLS

INGREDIENTS

CORNSTARCH	2 TABLESPOONS
	+ A LITTLE TO THICKEN THE SAUCE
WATER CHESTNUTS	4½ OZ (130 G)
SCALLIONS	3 STEMS
GINGER	¼ OZ (10 G)
GARLIC	¼ OZ (10 G)
GROUND PORK	1 LB 2 OZ (500 G)
EGG	1
SESAME OIL	1 TABLESPOON
WHITE PEPPER	2 PINCHES
OIL FOR FRYING	

SAUCE

SHAOXING WINE	⅓ CUP (80 ML)
OYSTER SAUCE	2 TABLESPOONS
LIGHT SOY SAUCE	1 TABLESPOON
WHITE SUGAR	2½ TABLESPOONS
STAR ANISE	1
BAY LEAF	1
CRUSHED GARLIC	1 TABLESPOON
WATER	⅔ CUP (150 ML)

❶ Combine all the sauce ingredients in a large pot and bring to a boil, then lower the heat and allow to reduce for 30 minutes until the liquid is about one-fifth of the original volume and the flavors are well balanced. ● Strain the aromatics and add a little cornstarch until the liquid thickens.

❷ Drain all the water from the chestnuts and chop them in a food processor. ● Finely chop the scallions, ginger, and garlic and add them to the food processor. ● Add the ground pork, egg, sesame oil, and white pepper and pulse to combine. ● Divide the mixture into 15 portions, each 1¾ oz (50 g). ● To form each meatball, throw it from one hand to the other, then roll it into a ball. ● This movement removes excess air and forms nice round meatballs.

❸ Coat the balls with the cornstarch. Heat a glug of oil in a frying pan over medium–high heat and fry the meatballs for about 3 minutes until browned. ● To finish, add the lion's head meatballs to the sauce in the pot, and simmer until the meatballs are fully cooked.

包子家族

孜然牛肉
CUMIN BEEF

SERVES 2

INGREDIENTS

BEEF SIRLOIN STEAK .... 9 OZ (250 G)
SALT ....1 PINCH
SHAOXING WINE ....1 TEASPOON
FISH SAUCE ....2 TEASPOONS
WHITE PEPPER ....1 TEASPOON
VEGETABLE OIL ....4 TEASPOONS
CORNSTARCH...1 TABLESPOON
EGG WHITE 1
CHOPPED GINGER ....1 TABLESPOON
CHOPPED GARLIC..1 TABLESPOON
CHOPPED FRESH CHILES 5

SPICY FERMENTED BEAN SAUCE
(DOU BAN JIANG) ....½ TABLESPOON
CUMIN SEEDS..1 TEASPOON
CILANTRO, CUT INTO ¼ INCH (5 MM) PIECES ....½ STEM
SESAME SEEDS..1 TEASPOON
OIL FOR FRYING

SAUCE

WHITE SUGAR ....1 TEASPOON
BLACK VINEGAR ....2 TEASPOONS
SHAOXING WINE ....2 TEASPOONS
LIGHT SOY SAUCE...2 TEASPOONS
CORNSTARCH...1 TABLESPOON

❶ Thinly slice the beef against the grain of the meat and place in a bowl. ● Add the salt, Shaoxing wine, fish sauce, white pepper, oil, cornstarch, and egg white, mix well, and set aside to marinate for 15 minutes.

❷ Heat a little oil in a frying pan over medium heat and fry the meat for about 30 seconds, stirring gently until each piece is browned. ● Remove the beef, set the meat aside, and reserve the oil in the pan.

❸ Prepare the sauce: in a small bowl, mix the sugar, black vinegar, wine, soy sauce, and cornstarch.

❹ Heat the frying pan containing a little of the beef frying oil over medium–high heat. ● Fry the ginger, garlic, chiles, and dou ban jiang until tender. ● Next add the beef and the sauce and stir for 10 seconds. ● Lastly, add the cumin seeds and cilantro. ● Garnish with the sesame seeds to serve.

包子家族

主菜

红烧茄子
HONGSHAO EGGPLANT

SERVES 2, AS A SIDE

INGREDIENTS

LEBANESE OR JAPANESE EGGPLANTS .... 9 OZ (250 G)
EGG 1
CORNSTARCH .... 1 TABLESPOON + 1 TEASPOON
LIGHT SOY SAUCE ....1 TABLESPOON
DARK SOY SAUCE ....1 TABLESPOON
SHAOXING WINE ....1 TABLESPOON
WHITE SUGAR ....2 TEASPOONS
WATER ....1 TABLESPOON
CHOPPED GINGER ....1 TEASPOON

CHOPPED GARLIC ....1 TEASPOON
CHOPPED FRESH CHILE ....2 TO 3 SMALL PIECES
SESAME OIL ....1 TEASPOON
OIL FOR COOKING AND FRYING

TO SERVE

SCALLION, CHOPPED ....1 SMALL
FRESH CHILE, CHOPPED ....½
TOASTED WHITE SESAME SEEDS ....1 TEASPOON

❶ Diagonally slice the eggplants into approximately 1 inch (2.5 cm) thick pieces, then place in a very large bowl. ● Break the egg into a small bowl and beat well. ● Pour the egg over the eggplants and mix until they are all well coated. ● Then add the 1 tablespoon of cornstarch, stirring carefully until all surfaces are evenly coated.

❷ Heat a 2 inch (5 cm) depth of oil in a pan to 325°F (160°C) and fry the eggplant slices in batches until lightly browned, with a nice even crust. ● Remove carefully and drain on paper towels to absorb excess oil.

❸ In a small bowl, mix the soy sauces, Shaoxing wine, and sugar. ● Stir until the sugar has dissolved. ● In a separate bowl, combine the 1 teaspoon of cornstarch and the measured water and mix until smooth and uniform.

❹ Heat a wok over medium–high heat and add 1 tablespoon of oil to coat the pan. ● Add the ginger and garlic, then stir for a few seconds.

❺ When they are fragrant but before they brown, add the soy sauce mixture and two or three small pieces of the fresh chile. ● When it starts to simmer, pour in the cornstarch and water mixture, then bring to a boil and stir until the sauce thickens slightly.

❻ Add the fried eggplant pieces and stir through the sauce until all the pieces are coated. ● Remove from the heat, add the sesame oil, and stir again.

❼ Serve on a plate, garnished with scallion, chile, and toasted sesame seeds.

包子家族

主
菜

香菇炒上海青
BOK CHOY AND SHIITAKE MUSHROOM STIR-FRY

SERVES 2, AS A SIDE

INGREDIENTS

DRIED SHIITAKE MUSHROOMS	2
BOK CHOY	1 LB 2 OZ (500 G)
BAKING SODA	1 PINCH
VEGETABLE OIL	1 TABLESPOON + A FEW DROPS
DARK SOY SAUCE	1 TEASPOON + 1 TABLESPOON

CHOPPED GARLIC	1 TEASPOON
SALT	1 PINCH
OYSTER SAUCE	1 TEASPOON
CORNSTARCH AND WATER MIXTURE (1:3 CORNSTARCH TO WATER RATIO)	1 TABLESPOON
SESAME SEEDS	1 PINCH

1 Soak the shiitake mushrooms in water for 20 minutes to rehydrate them, then drain, rinse, and thinly slice them. ● Soak the bok choy in water with the baking soda (this will remove impurities that can be found at the root of the vegetable). ● Drain, then cut it into quarters lengthways (or sixths, if large).

2 Immerse the lower part of the bok choy in boiling water for 1 minute while holding the green leaves in your hand, then let it go completely into the water. ● Leave to cook for 1½ to 2 minutes, then refresh in iced water to stop it from cooking further.

3 Pour the 1 tablespoon of oil into a frying pan over medium–high heat together with the shiitake mushrooms and the 1 teaspoon of soy sauce. ● Stir for 1 minute, then add the garlic. ● Add the bok choy and fry for 30 seconds. ● Add the salt, oyster sauce, the remaining soy sauce, and the cornstarch and water mixture.

4 Cook until the sauce thickens, remove from the heat, then add a few drops of oil. ● Garnish with sesame seeds and serve immediately.

包
子
家
族

主菜

干煸四季豆
SICHUAN
GREEN BEANS

THIS RECIPE IS TRADITIONALLY MADE WITH FLAT GREEN BEANS (OR ROMANO BEANS).
WE ADAPTED THE RECIPE TO USE FRENCH GREEN BEANS BECAUSE THE SEASON WAS PARTICULARLY ABUNDANT.
MAKE SURE YOU ADJUST THE COOKING TIME ACCORDING TO THE SIZE OF THE BEANS.

SERVES 2, AS A SIDE

INGREDIENTS

GREEN BEANS .... 1 LB 2 OZ (500 G)
GROUND PORK .... 2 OZ (60 G)
MINCED GINGER .... 2 TEASPOONS
CHOPPED GARLIC .... 2 TEASPOONS
GROUND RED SICHUAN PEPPER .... 1 TEASPOON

WHOLE DRIED CHILES 3
LIGHT SOY SAUCE .... 2 TABLESPOONS
WHITE SUGAR .... 1 TEASPOON
BLACK VINEGAR .... 1 TEASPOON
VEGETABLE OIL FOR FRYING

❶ Heat a drizzle of oil in a large frying pan over medium–high heat and fry the beans for 35 to 40 seconds, until they take on a slightly rough texture. ● Remove from the pan and set aside.

❷ Pour a drizzle more oil into the frying pan, then fry the ground pork until the meat is nicely browned. ● Add the ginger, garlic, Sichuan pepper, and chiles to the meat, then return the beans to the pan. ● Stir-fry quickly, pour in the soy sauce, sugar, and black vinegar, stir again, and serve immediately.

包子家族

豆芽炒韭菜
BEAN SPROUTS WITH GARLIC CHIVES

SERVES 2, AS A SIDE

INGREDIENTS			
GARLIC CHIVES	5½ OZ (150 G)	VEGETABLE OIL	A DRIZZLE
GARLIC	1 CLOVE	BEAN SPROUTS	14 OZ (400 G)
GINGER	1 SMALL PIECE	OYSTER SAUCE	1 TEASPOON
		SALT	1 PINCH

❶ Cut the chives into 2 inch (5 cm) pieces, then peel and chop the garlic and ginger.

❷ Heat the vegetable oil in a large frying pan over medium–high heat and fry the garlic and ginger. ● Before they start to brown, add the bean sprouts and stir-fry for 30 to 60 seconds. ● Add the garlic chives and stir-fry again for 30 seconds. ● Season with the oyster sauce and salt. ● Stir-fry again for 30 to 60 seconds. ● Serve.

主菜

清炒空心菜
STIR-FRIED WATER SPINACH

SERVES 2, AS A SIDE

INGREDIENTS

WATER SPINACH..1 LB 2 OZ (500 G)
VEGETABLE OIL ....A DRIZZLE
GARLIC, SLICED...2 CLOVES

OYSTER SAUCE ....1 TABLESPOON
OR VEGETABLE STOCK + SOY SAUCE.................⅓ CUP (80 ML)

包子家族

❶ Rinse the water spinach well. ● Holding the stems together, cut off the leaves and set them aside, then cut the stems into 3 to 4 inch (8 to 10 cm) lengths and set them aside separately.

❷ Pour a drizzle of vegetable oil into a frying pan over medium–high heat and add the garlic. ● When the garlic releases its aromas, scatter the water spinach stems into the pan. ● After about 1 minute, stir the stems. ● After 1 to 2 minutes, once the stems have started to soften, add the leaves. ● Add the oyster sauce, or the vegetable stock seasoned with soy sauce. ● Cook, stirring, for 1 minute, until the leaves are tender. ● Serve immediately.

主菜

蒜蓉炒芥兰
STIR-FRIED CHINESE BROCCOLI

SERVES 2, AS A SIDE

INGREDIENTS

CHINESE BROCCOLI	1 LB 2 OZ (500 G)
RED BELL PEPPER	1¾ OZ (50 G)
VEGETABLE OIL	1 TABLESPOON
FINELY SLICED GARLIC	1 LARGE CLOVE
CHOPPED GINGER	1 TEASPOON
SALT	1 TEASPOON
WHITE SUGAR	½ TEASPOON
OYSTER SAUCE	1 TEASPOON
CORNSTARCH AND WATER MIXTURE (1:3 CORNSTARCH TO WATER RATIO)	1 TABLESPOON
SESAME OIL	A FEW DROPS
SHAOXING WINE	A FEW DROPS

❶ Peel the fibrous outer layer of the broccoli stems. ● Cut the broccoli into quarters lengthways. ● Cut the bell pepper into thin matchsticks.

❷ Boil the broccoli in salted boiling water until cooked but still crunchy. ● Meanwhile, prepare a bowl of iced water to refresh the broccoli and stop it from cooking further. Drain well.

❸ Heat the vegetable oil in a frying pan over medium–high heat. ● Add the garlic and ginger. ● Once aromatic, add the broccoli and stir. ● Add the salt, sugar, and bell pepper. ● Stir-fry for 1 minute, then stir in the oyster sauce and the cornstarch and water mixture.

❹ Once the sauce has thickened slightly and the broccoli is fully coated, pour in the sesame oil and Shaoxing wine, stir one last time, and serve.

VARIATION

To make a vegetarian version, omit the oyster sauce and add a little more sugar and salt instead.

包子家族

主菜

炒土豆絲
STIR-FRIED SHREDDED POTATO
TU DOU SI

SERVES 2, AS A SIDE

INGREDIENTS

WAXY POTATOES	14 OZ (400 G)
GREEN AND RED BELL PEPPER	1¾ OZ (50 G)
VEGETABLE OIL	1½ TABLESPOONS
FINELY SLICED GARLIC	2 LARGE CLOVES
GINGER, CUT INTO MATCHSTICKS	1 INCH (2.5 CM) PIECE
SALT	1 TEASPOON
OYSTER SAUCE	1 TEASPOON
WHITE SUGAR	1 TEASPOON
RICE VINEGAR	1 TABLESPOON
CHOPPED SCALLIONS	1 SMALL HANDFUL

❶ Wash and peel the potatoes. ● Cut the base of each potato so you have a flat surface to work with. ● Cut into approximately ¹⁄₁₆ inch (1.5 mm) slices. ● Spread the slices out, overlapping them slightly, then cut them into ¹⁄₁₆ inch (1.5 mm) thick matchsticks. ● If the potatoes are very large, you can shorten the length to 2½ inches (6 cm). ● Immerse them in iced water, drain, and rinse until the water is clear. ● Soak in room-temperature water for 5 minutes, then drain. ● Cut the bell peppers into thin matchsticks and soak them separately in water.

❷ Heat a large frying pan and pour in the oil. ● When it starts smoking, turn off the heat and fry the garlic and ginger until lightly golden, then add the potatoes and fry for 1 minute over medium–high heat.

❸ Add the salt, oyster sauce, and drained bell peppers and fry for 2 minutes. ● Lastly, add the sugar and rice vinegar. ● Fry until there is nearly no liquid left in the pan. ● The potatoes should be glossy but not browned. ● Garnish with chopped scallions.

包子家族

主菜

炒莲白
STIR-FRIED CABBAGE

SERVES 2

INGREDIENTS

GREEN CABBAGE .... 10½ OZ (300 G)
VEGETABLE OIL .... 2 TABLESPOONS
CHOPPED GARLIC .... 1 TEASPOON
CHOPPED GINGER .... 1 TEASPOON
DRIED RED CHILES 3
SICHUAN RED PEPPERS .... 4 TO 5
WATER .... SCANT ½ CUP (100 ML)
WHITE SUGAR .... ½ TEASPOON

SAUCE

SHAOXING WINE .... 2 TABLESPOONS
LIGHT SOY SAUCE .... 1 TABLESPOON
BLACK VINEGAR .... 1 TABLESPOON

包子家族

❶ Roughly tear the cabbage leaves by hand. ● Prepare the sauce by mixing the Shaoxing wine, soy sauce, and black vinegar in a bowl.

❷ In a wok over medium–high heat, heat the oil and stir-fry the garlic, ginger, dried chiles, and Sichuan peppers until aromatic. ● Add the cabbage and stir for 1 minute. ● Pour in the sauce and water, then stir for 2 to 3 minutes until the cabbage starts to soften. ● Add the sugar and stir over high heat for 1 minute. ● Serve.

主菜

韭菜炒鸡蛋
SCRAMBLED EGGS WITH GARLIC CHIVES

FOR THIS RECIPE NO ADDITIONAL SEASONING IS NEEDED—JUST ALLOW THE SUBTLE FLAVORS OF THE GARLIC CHIVES AND EGGS TO EXPLODE IN YOUR MOUTH.

SERVES 2

INGREDIENTS

EGGS 4
SALT .... 2 PINCHES
GROUND BLACK PEPPER .... 1 PINCH
GARLIC CHIVES .... 10½ OZ (300 G)
CORNSTARCH .... 1 PINCH
VEGETABLE OIL .... 3 TABLESPOONS + A FEW DROPS

❶ Break the eggs into a bowl and add 1 pinch of salt and the ground pepper. ● Beat well.

❷ Trim the roots of the garlic chives, then cut them into 1½ to 2 inch (4 to 5 cm) pieces. ● Add 1 pinch of salt and the cornstarch and mix gently.

❸ Heat 2 tablespoons of the oil in a frying pan over medium–high heat until it starts smoking. ● Lower the heat and immediately pour in the beaten eggs. ● Raise the heat to high and stir so that the entire surface is covered with egg. ● Gently unstick the omelet from the pan with a spatula if necessary. ● Once the omelet starts to brown, flip it over. ● Add 1 tablespoon of oil to the edges, continue stirring, and then flip it over again. ● Using a spatula, break the omelet into large pieces.

❹ Add the garlic chives and fry for 1 minute, stirring rapidly. ● The garlic chives will wilt and take on a bright green color. ● Add a few drops of oil, mix, then serve.

包子家族

主菜

麻婆豆腐
MAPO TOFU

SERVES 2

INGREDIENTS

TOFU	1 LB 2 OZ (500 G)
VEGETABLE OIL	2 TABLESPOONS
GROUND PORK	3½ OZ (100 G)
MINCED GINGER	1 TEASPOON
MINCED GARLIC	1 TEASPOON
GROUND RED SICHUAN PEPPER	1 TEASPOON
CHILE POWDER	1 TEASPOON
SPICY FERMENTED BEAN SAUCE (DOU BAN JIANG)	1 TABLESPOON
FERMENTED BLACK BEANS (DOUCHI)	½ TABLESPOON
SLICED FRESH RED CHILE	1
DARK SOY SAUCE	½ TABLESPOON
WHITE SUGAR	½ TABLESPOON
WATER	3½ TABLESPOONS
CORNSTARCH AND WATER MIXTURE (1:3 CORNSTARCH TO WATER RATIO)	3 TABLESPOONS
SLICED SCALLIONS TO GARNISH	

❶ Cut the block of tofu into ¾ inch (2 cm) cubes and cook in salted boiling water for 1 minute. ● Drain.

❷ Pour 1 tablespoon of the vegetable oil into a wok, add the ground pork, and fry for about 1 minute until nicely browned. ● Remove and set aside.

❸ Add 1 tablespoon of the vegetable oil to the same wok. ● Fry the following ingredients in this order, frying each one until tender before adding the next: ginger and garlic, Sichuan red pepper, chile powder, dou ban jiang, fermented black beans, fresh chile, soy sauce, and finally the sugar. ● Stir until the sauce is smooth, aromatic, and slightly red in color. ● Then add the pork and tofu and pour in the water.

❹ Simmer for 1 to 2 minutes, stirring the tofu cubes occasionally with the back of a spoon so as not to break them. ● Add the cornstarch and water mixture, 1 tablespoon at a time, then let it thicken. ● Once all ingredients are well heated through, serve, garnished with scallions.

VARIATION

To make a vegetarian version, use rehydrated shiitake mushrooms instead of the pork.

包子家族

米饭和面条

RICE
& NOODLES
223

米饭和面条

广东炒饭
CANTONESE FRIED RICE

THERE ARE MANY WAYS TO MAKE FRIED RICE. THIS IS A LIGHT RECIPE THAT USES UP
LEFTOVER VEGETABLES, WHICH IN OUR CASE TURNED OUT TO BE LEEKS AND CHOY SUM STALKS.
YOU'LL GET A BETTER RESULT USING RICE WITH THE GRAINS ALREADY SEPARATED,
AND IDEALLY, RICE COOKED THE PREVIOUS DAY.

SERVES 2

INGREDIENTS

EGGS	3
VEGETABLE OIL	½ CUP (120 ML)
CHOPPED GARLIC	2 TEASPOONS
CHOPPED GINGER	1 TEASPOON
SLICED LEEKS	5½ OZ (150 G)
LEFTOVER COOKED CHOY SUM	7 OZ (200 G)
COOKED WHITE RICE	2¾ CUPS (400 G)
SALT	2 PINCHES
GROUND BLACK PEPPER	2 PINCHES
WHITE SUGAR	1 PINCH
DARK SOY SAUCE	2 TABLESPOONS
SCALLIONS, CHOPPED	2 STEMS

❶ Beat the eggs in a bowl. ● Pour the oil into a hot frying pan (the amount may seem high, but this will result in aerated eggs and flavorful rice). ● Pour the eggs into the oil and stir. ● Cook over high heat for 20 seconds until the eggs are set, then add the garlic and ginger and stir again.

❷ Add the sliced leeks and fry for 1 minute, then add the leftover choy sum. ● Next add the rice and alternate between stirring and allowing the rice to heat through. ● Finally, add the salt, pepper, sugar, dark soy sauce, and a little chopped scallion. ● Stir so that all ingredients are well combined.

❸ Serve, garnished with the remaining scallion.

包子家族

米饭和面条

蔬菜炒面
STIR-FRIED VEGETABLE NOODLES

SERVES 2

INGREDIENTS

WHEAT NOODLES	9 OZ (250 G)
DRIED SHIITAKE MUSHROOMS	3
GARLIC SCAPES	2
BOK CHOY	2
VEGETABLE OIL	2 TABLESPOONS

MINCED GARLIC	2 TEASPOONS
CHOPPED GINGER	2 TEASPOONS
LIGHT SOY SAUCE	2 TABLESPOONS
DARK SOY SAUCE	3 TABLESPOONS
BEAN SPROUTS	⅓ CUP (60 G)

❶ Cook the noodles according to the package instructions, drain, and allow to cool. ● Soak the shiitake mushrooms in water for 20 minutes to rehydrate them, then drain, reserving about 3½ tablespoons of the soaking water. Cut the mushrooms into strips. ● If the garlic scapes are thick, cook them in salted boiling water for 1 to 2 minutes (otherwise, you can add them directly to the noodles). ● Cut off the bok choy roots and separate the leaves.

❷ Add the oil to hot pan and fry the garlic, ginger, and mushrooms in the oil. ● Stir for 30 seconds, then add the bok choy and garlic scapes.

● Mix again. ● Pour in the reserved mushroom soaking water and cook for 30 seconds.

❸ Add the noodles and soy sauces and stir-fry energetically until all the sauce is well distributed and noodles are heated through. ● Finally add the bean sprouts, stir one last time, and serve immediately.

包子家族

米饭和面条

干炒牛河
STIR-FRIED RICE NOODLES WITH BEEF HO FUN

SERVES 2

INGREDIENTS

THICK RICE NOODLES	14 OZ (400 G)
BEEF (LIKE SKIRT STEAK)	7 OZ (200 G)
ONION	½
SCALLION	1 OZ (30 G)
EGGS	2
OYSTER SAUCE	1 TABLESPOON
BEAN SPROUTS	3½ OZ (100 G)
DARK SOY SAUCE	1 TABLESPOON
OIL FOR COOKING	

MARINADE

DARK SOY SAUCE	1½ TABLESPOONS
LIGHT SOY SAUCE	¾ TABLESPOON
OYSTER SAUCE	1 TABLESPOON
VEGETABLE OIL	½ TEASPOON
WHITE PEPPER	1 PINCH
WHITE SUGAR	2 TEASPOONS
WATER	2 TEASPOONS

SAUCE

DARK SOY SAUCE	1½ TABLESPOONS
LIGHT SOY SAUCE	½ TABLESPOON
WHITE SUGAR	1 TABLESPOON

❶ Soak the rice noodles in hot water for 20 minutes (the water should not be boiling).

❷ Meanwhile, prepare the marinade by mixing all the ingredients together in a large bowl. ● Thinly slice the beef against the grain of the meat, then add the meat to the marinade and leave to marinate for at least 15 minutes.

❸ Prepare the sauce by mixing the soy sauces and sugar together. Set aside.

❹ Cut the onion into strips, cut the scallion into 2 inch (5 cm) lengths, and beat the eggs in a bowl.

❺ In a hot oiled wok, cook the eggs for 2 minutes, then add the noodles and cook for 2 minutes until the texture begins to change. ● Next, add the oyster sauce and sauce ingredients, then stir for 30 seconds. ● Add the bean sprouts at the last minute and cook for 30 seconds. ● Divide the noodles among bowls (or place in a serving dish).

❻ Add more oil to the wok, then brown the onion. ● Next add the beef, scallion, and dark soy sauce. Fry for 30 seconds until beef is cooked but still tender.

❼ Serve on the bed of noodles.

包子家族

米饭和面条

葱油拌面
SHANGHAI NOODLES WITH SCALLION

ENOUGH SAUCE FOR AROUND 15 SERVINGS

INGREDIENTS

FRESH NOODLES ....5½ OZ (150 G) PER SERVING

SAUCE

SCALLIONS .... 7 OZ (200 G)
VEGETABLE OIL .... 1¼ CUPS (300 ML) + FOR FRYING
RED ASIAN SHALLOTS ....3¼ OZ (90 G)
DRIED SHRIMP ....¾ OZ (20 G)
LIGHT SOY SAUCE ....⅓ CUP (90 ML)
DARK SOY SAUCE .... ¾ CUP (180 ML)

WATER...1 CUP (230 ML)
CILANTRO... 4 STEMS
FINELY SLICED GINGER ....2 TABLESPOONS
CARROTS, FINELY CHOPPED.......................5½ OZ (150 G)
WHITE SUGAR ....2 TABLESPOONS

GARNISH

SCALLIONS, CHOPPED

❶ Cut the scallion stems, separating the whites from the greens, then fry them separately in oil until tender. ● Set aside, keeping them separate. ● Cut the shallots into strips, fry them in the same oil, then set aside. ● Lastly, fry the dried shrimp in the same oil, drain the infused oil, and set it aside (nothing is discarded).

❷ In a pot, combine the soy sauces, water, cilantro, ginger, carrot, half the fried shallots, and half the fried shrimp, and simmer over medium heat for 20 minutes. ● Pass through a sieve, discarding the aromatics, add the sugar, and reduce until a sauce consistency is reached.

❸ Add the 1¼ cups (300 ml) oil to the slightly reduced sauce and bring just to a boil. ● Turn off the heat and add a little of the green parts of the scallions, along with the other half of the fried shrimp, then allow to cool (the sauce can be stored in the refrigerator for 1 week).

❹ Cook the noodles according to package instructions in salted boiling water until they are al dente. ● Heat about ⅓ cup (80 ml) of sauce per serving and stir it through the drained noodles with some fried white parts of the scallions.

❺ Garnish with the remaining fried shallots and scallion greens, as well as chopped fresh scallions.

包子家族

米饭和面条

炸酱面
ZHAJIANG NOODLES

SERVES 2

INGREDIENTS

PORK BELLY .... 3½ OZ (100 G)
VEGETABLE OIL .... A DRIZZLE
CHOPPED GARLIC .... 1 TEASPOON
CHOPPED GINGER .... 1 TEASPOON
FERMENTED YELLOW SOYBEAN PASTE
(HUANGDOU JIANG) .... 1 TABLESPOON
DRY YELLOW SOYBEAN PASTE
(GAN HUANG JIANG) .... 1 TABLESPOON
SWEET FERMENTED BEAN SAUCE
(TIAN MIAN JIANG) .... 4 TEASPOONS

SHAOXING WINE .... 2 TABLESPOONS
WATER .... SCANT 1 CUP (200 ML)
FRESH WHEAT NOODLES (WITHOUT EGGS) .... 9 OZ (250 G)
CARROT, CUT INTO MATCHSTICKS .... 1¾ OZ (50 G)
SHELLED EDAMAME BEANS .... ⅓ CUP (50 G)
DAIKON, CUT INTO MATCHSTICKS .... 1¾ OZ (50 G)
CUCUMBER, CUT INTO MATCHSTICKS .... 1¾ OZ (50 G)
CILANTRO SPRIGS TO GARNISH

❶ Cut the pork belly into small cubes and fry until brown in a wok with the oil, garlic, and ginger. ● Add the bean pastes and sauce and stir for 1 minute. ● Pour in the Shaoxing wine and water, then cook for about 7 minutes until it is reduced by half.

❷ Cook the noodles in salted boiling water according to the package instructions. ● Transfer immediately to a bowl of iced water to refresh and stop them from cooking further. ● Meanwhile, cook the carrot, edamame, and daikon separately in salted boiling water for 1 minute and transfer to iced water, keeping them separate. Drain.

❸ Divide the noodles into bowls or plates, pour a ladleful of meat sauce into the middle, then arrange the cooked vegetables and cucumber all around the sauce. Garnish with a sprig of cilantro and serve.

包子家族

米饭和面条

担担面
DAN DAN NOODLES

SERVES 2

INGREDIENTS

SICHUAN RED PEPPERS	¼ OZ (10 G)
DRIED CHILE FLAKES	7 TABLESPOONS (40 G)
PEANUTS	¾ OZ (20 G)
GROUND PORK	4¼ OZ (120 G)
CHOPPED SCALLIONS	1 CUP (60 G)
SALT	1½ TEASPOONS + FOR COOKING
WHEAT NOODLES	9 OZ (250 G)
BOK CHOY, QUARTERED	2 OZ (60 G)
SESAME PASTE (ZHI MA JIANG)	4 TEASPOONS
LIGHT SOY SAUCE	¼ CUP (60 ML)
VINEGAR	2 TABLESPOONS
WHITE SUGAR	2½ TEASPOONS

SESAME OIL	1 TEASPOON
PRESERVED MUSTARD GREENS (YA CAI)	1 OZ (30 G)
VEGETABLE OIL FOR FRYING	

GARNISH

SCALLIONS, CHOPPED	3 STEMS
JULIENNED CARROT	
JULIENNED CUCUMBER	

❶ Add a drizzle of oil to a hot frying pan and fry the Sichuan red peppers over medium–high heat for 8 to 10 minutes until the seeds start to brown. ● Lower the heat and stir in the chile flakes. ● Remove from the pan and leave to cool.

❷ In a clean frying pan, fry the peanuts over medium–high heat, then remove and crush them.

❸ Pour a drizzle of oil into the frying pan over medium–high heat and fry the ground pork and scallions. ● Season with a little salt and set aside.

❹ Cook the noodles in boiling salted water according to the package instructions, adding the bok choy 1 minute before the end of cooking. ● Drain, reserving 1 teaspoon of the cooking water, and transfer to a bowl. ● In another bowl, mix the sesame paste, reserved noodle cooking water, soy sauce, vinegar, sugar, measured salt, and sesame oil. ● Pour the sauce over the noodles, sprinkle with ya cai and crushed peanuts, and add the pork. ● Strain the cooled chile oil and drizzle over the noodles. ● Garnish with the scallions, carrot, and cucumber and serve.

包子家族

米饭和面条

麻酱面
COLD NOODLES WITH SESAME

SERVES 2

INGREDIENTS

CARROT	3½ OZ (100 G)
CUCUMBER	3½ OZ (100 G)
BEAN SPROUTS	⅓ CUP (60 G)
FRESH NOODLES (WITHOUT EGGS)	10½ OZ (300 G)
CILANTRO	3 SPRIGS (STEMS AND LEAVES)
WHITE SESAME SEEDS	2 PINCHES

SAUCE

SESAME PASTE (ZHI MA JIANG)	3½ TABLESPOONS
SESAME OIL	2 TEASPOONS
PEANUT BUTTER	HEAPED 1 TABLESPOON
LIGHT SOY SAUCE	4 TEASPOONS
BLACK VINEGAR	4 TEASPOONS
MIRIN	1 TABLESPOON
WHITE RICE VINEGAR	1 TABLESPOON

❶ Cut the carrot and cucumber into thin matchsticks, wash the bean sprouts, and set aside.

❷ Cook the noodles in boiling salted water according to the package instructions and then refresh in iced water.

❸ In a large bowl, mix all the sauce ingredients together with a handheld immersion blender or whisk. ● If using a whisk, first mix the sesame paste and sesame oil with the peanut butter, before gradually adding the liquid ingredients.

❹ Add the noodles to the sauce and mix until well coated.

❺ Serve the noodles in a bowl topped with the fresh vegetables, cilantro, and sesame seeds.

包子家族

甜点

DESSERTS
243

甜点

黑芝麻包
BLACK SESAME BAO

MAKES AROUND 12 BAO

INGREDIENTS

BLACK SESAME SEEDS .... 1¾ CUPS (255 G)
WHITE SESAME SEEDS .... ½ TABLESPOON
BUTTER .... ½ CUP (125 G)

HONEY .... ½ CUP (150 G)
BAOZI DOUGH (PAGE 86) .... 1 RECIPE
SALT .... 1 PINCH
OIL FOR FRYING (OPTIONAL)

❶ Toast the sesame seeds in a dry frying pan or oven until the white sesame seeds are golden brown. ● Allow to cool, reserve 1 tablespoon for garnishing, then grind them in a blender (a finely ground blend will give the filling a better consistency and avoid getting as many sesame seeds stuck in your teeth after eating!).

❷ Melt the butter in a saucepan, then add the sesame seeds and honey. ● Stir until well combined and then set aside to cool in the refrigerator. ● When the mixture is solid but still soft enough to shape, form it into twelve 1¼ oz (35 g) balls.

❸ Assemble according to the step-by-step instructions on pages 86–89. ● Each bao should use 1¾ oz (50 g) dough and one 1¼ oz (35 g) ball of filling.

● Let the bao rise for the second time in a warm, humid place for 20 minutes. ● Steam for 12 minutes and serve immediately.

❹ Bao can be eaten once removed from the steamer. ● However, for our Bao Family signature Sesame Bao, fry the bottom of the bao in oil until you get a beautiful golden color (make sure the bottom is tightly closed to prevent any filling spilling into the hot oil). ● Serve sprinkled with the reserved sesame seeds and a pinch of salt on top.

TIP

You can use any leftover baozi dough to make Mantou (page 50).

包子家族

甜
点

紅豆沙包
RED BEAN BAO

THIS RECIPE USES TRADITIONAL RED BEAN PASTE, WHICH IS TYPICALLY VERY SWEET,
FLAVORED WITH LEMON AND SPICES. IT IS VERY SIMPLE, SUPER ADDICTIVE, AND IT MAKES
A VERY GOOD BAO FOR DESSERT OR TO SERVE AS A SNACK AT ROOM TEMPERATURE.

MAKES AROUND 12 BAO

INGREDIENTS

BUTTER	14 TABLESPOONS (200 G)
WATER	2⅔ TABLESPOONS
RED BEAN PASTE	1½ CUPS (500 G)
CONDENSED MILK	⅔ CUP (160 ML)
FRESHLY GROUND TIMUT PEPPER (OPTIONAL)	1 PINCH
GRATED LEMON ZEST	FROM 1 LEMON
BAOZI DOUGH (PAGE 86)	1 RECIPE

❶ Melt the butter in a saucepan, then pour in the water, red bean paste, condensed milk, ground timut pepper (if using), and grated lemon zest. ● Stir until well combined, heating over low heat if necessary, then leave to cool in the refrigerator. ● When the mixture is solid but still soft enough to shape, form it into twelve 1¼ oz (35 g) balls.

❷ Assemble according to the step-by-step instructions on pages 86–89. ● Each bao should use 1¾ oz (50 g) dough and one 1½ oz (40 g) ball of filling. ● Let the bao rise for the second time in a warm, humid place for 20 minutes. ● Steam for 12 minutes and serve immediately.

TIPS

Bao can be eaten as soon as they come out of the steamer or served at room temperature. ● You can use any leftover baozi dough to make Mantou (page 50).

包
子
家
族

甜点

流沙包
FLOWING SAND BAO

MAKES AROUND 24 BAO

INGREDIENTS

SALTED DUCK EGG YOLKS 6
AGAR-AGAR .... 2½ TABLESPOONS (12 G)
CORNSTARCH.. ½ CUP (60 G)
WHITE SUGAR ....1 CUP (200 G)

COCONUT MILK .... GENEROUS 2 CUPS (500 ML)
HEAVY CREAM...1 CUP (240 ML)
BUTTER ....¼ CUP (60 G)
BAOZI DOUGH (PAGE 86) ....2 RECIPES

❶ Steam the egg yolks for 12 minutes, then crush using a fork. ● In a blender (or in a tall container, using an immersion blender), blend the egg yolks, agar-agar, cornstarch, and 1 heaped tablespoon of the sugar.

❷ In a deep pot, heat the coconut milk, heavy cream, and remaining sugar, without letting it boil.

❸ Transfer about a third of the hot liquid to the blender containing the yolk mixture, and blend until smooth. ● Transfer the mixture to the pot and cook over medium–low heat, stirring with a spatula to ensure the bottom doesn't stick. ● Once the mixture has thickened, transfer to a large bowl.

❹ Cut the butter into cubes, then stir it into the mixture, piece by piece. ● If the butter remains separated, mix with a whisk to incorporate. ● Allow to cool completely.

❺ Assemble according to the step-by-step instructions on pages 86–89. ● Each bao should use 1¾ oz (50 g) dough and 1½ oz (40 g) of filling. ● Let the bao rise for the second time in a warm, humid place for 20 minutes. ● Steam for 10 minutes and serve immediately.

TIP

You can use any leftover baozi dough to make Mantou (page 50).

包子家族

甜点

蛋挞
EGG TARTS

MAKES AROUND 15 TARTS

FILLING	
WHITE SUGAR	SCANT ½ CUP (85 G)
HOT WATER	SCANT 1 CUP (200 ML)
EGGS	3 LARGE (150 G)
EVAPORATED MILK	½ CUP (120 ML)
VANILLA EXTRACT	1 TEASPOON

DOUGH	
SOFTENED BUTTER	10 TABLESPOONS (150 G)
CONFECTIONERS' SUGAR	½ CUP (50 G)
EGG, BEATEN	1
MILK POWDER	1½ TABLESPOONS
ALL-PURPOSE FLOUR	2 CUPS (250 G)
SALT	⅓ TEASPOON

❶ Prepare the filling: dissolve the sugar in the hot water. ● Beat the eggs with the evaporated milk and vanilla extract, then add the mixture to the sugar liquid. ● Pass through a fine sieve to remove all air bubbles. ● Set aside.

❷ Prepare the dough: beat the butter with the confectioners' sugar until a creamy, airy texture is obtained. ● Add the beaten egg, followed by the dry ingredients. ● Mix with your hands until a dough forms, but be careful not to overwork it to prevent it from becoming too dense. ● Allow it to cool in the refrigerator until it has a play-dough–like consistency.

❸ Preheat the oven to 375°F (190°C). ● Divide the dough into 15 portions, each about 1¼ oz (35 g). Using your thumb, press each portion into the base of a 3 inch (8 cm) tart pan, or a muffin pan with 3 inch (8 cm) cups. ● Pour the filling in to come halfway up the sides.

❹ Bake for 6 minutes, then lower the temperature to 325°F (165°C) to finish cooking: the egg mixture must be cooked and lightly puffed, and the crust lightly browned.

包子家族

汤圆
TANGYUAN

MAKES AROUND 18 TANGYUAN

FILLING

COCONUT OIL, PORK FAT, OR BUTTER	7 TABLESPOONS (100 G)
BLACK SESAME SEEDS, CRUSHED	⅔ CUP (100 G)
WHITE SUGAR	⅔ CUP (125 G)
PEANUT BUTTER	⅓ CUP (100 G)
SESAME OIL	1 TEASPOON

DOUGH

GLUTINOUS (STICKY) RICE FLOUR	1⅓ CUPS (160 G)
RICE FLOUR	2¼ TABLESPOONS
WATER	GENEROUS ½ CUP (140 ML)
WHITE SUGAR	1½ TABLESPOONS
VEGETABLE OIL	4 TEASPOONS

GINGER SYRUP

SLICED GINGER	1½ TABLESPOONS
RAW SUGAR	½ CUP (100 G)
WATER	2¾ CUPS (650 ML)

❶ Prepare the syrup: combine all the ingredients in a saucepan and simmer for 10 minutes. Set aside.

❷ Prepare the filling: bring the fat to room temperature to make it easier to work with. ● In a large bowl, use a spoon to mix the fat with the remaining filling ingredients. ● Form into about eighteen ⅛ oz (6 g) balls and refrigerate until firm.

❸ Prepare the dough: mix all the ingredients together until a smooth dough is obtained. ● Divide the dough into about eighteen ¾ oz (20 g) balls.

❹ To assemble, form a hollow in the center of each dough ball with your thumb and insert a ball of filling. ● Wrap the dough around the filling, then roll using your hands to form a smooth ball.

❺ Drop the tangyuan into a large pot of boiling water and cook for about 2 minutes until they begin to rise to the surface. Once risen to the surface, let them cook for another 1 to 2 minutes.

❻ Drain and serve in the ginger syrup.

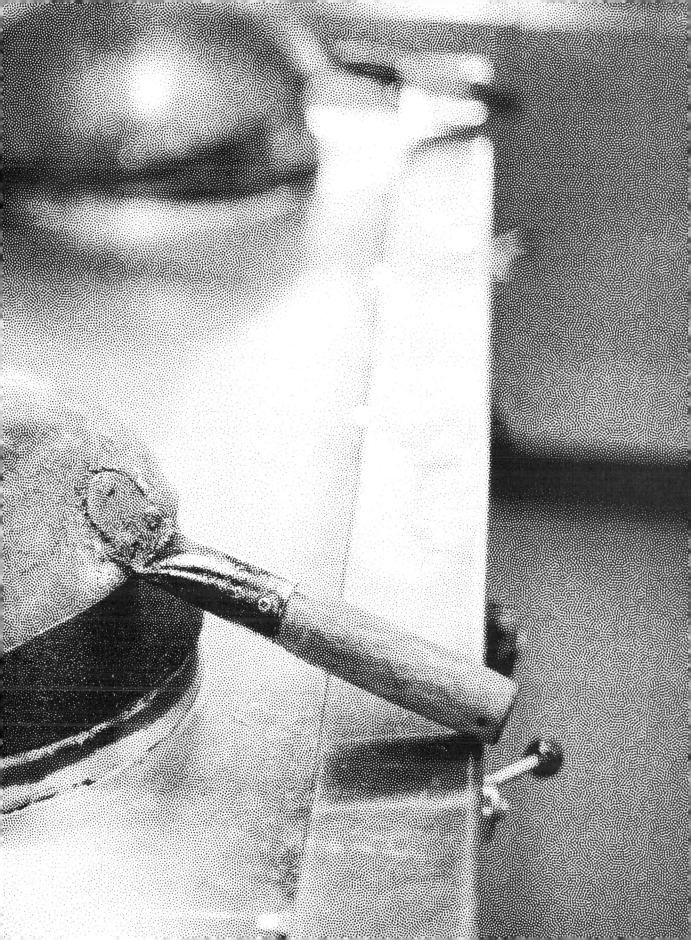

西多士
HONG KONG FRENCH TOAST

SERVES 2

INGREDIENTS

PEANUT BUTTER .... ¼ CUP (60 ML)
SANDWICH BREAD, CRUSTS REMOVED .... 4 SLICES
VEGETABLE OIL .... ¾ CUP (180 ML)
EGGS 3

GARNISH

BUTTER .... 2 TABLESPOONS
MAPLE SYRUP .... ¼ CUP (60 ML)

❶ Spread the peanut butter on a slice of bread and cover with another slice of bread to form a sandwich. ● Repeat with the other two slices.

❷ In a deep pan, heat the oil to 350°F (180°C). ● Meanwhile, beat the eggs well, then pour them into a shallow bowl.

❸ Dip one sandwich at a time into the beaten egg, making sure all sides are covered. ● Gently place the sandwich in the hot oil and fry it for 2 minutes until you get a nice golden color on both sides (the oil should be hot enough to lightly puff up the egg).

❹ Serve with butter and maple syrup.

炸鲜奶
FRIED MILK

SERVES 2

INGREDIENTS

MILK	1 CUP (250 ML)
CORNSTARCH	½ CUP (60 G)
WHITE SUGAR	1½ TABLESPOONS
CONDENSED MILK	4 TEASPOONS
BAKING POWDER	2½ TEASPOONS
WATER	SCANT ½ CUP (100 ML)
VEGETABLE OIL	
ALL-PURPOSE FLOUR FOR COATING	

❶ In a saucepan, heat the milk, ¼ cup (30 g) of the cornstarch, and the sugar and condensed milk over low heat, stirring continuously until the mixture thickens. ● Transfer to a small lightly oiled rectangular dish or container (the mixture should be about 1 inch/3 cm deep). Leave to cool in the refrigerator for at least 1 hour.

❷ In a large pot, heat a 2 inch (5 cm) depth of oil to to 325°F (160°C). ● Meanwhile, cut the milk mixture into ¾ × 2 inch (2 × 5 cm) rectangles and coat the whole surface of each with flour. ● Prepare the coating by mixing the remaining cornstarch, baking powder, and water. ● Dip each milk rectangle in the coating, then carefully place them into the oil. ● Fry until the pieces are nice and golden. ● Transfer to paper towels to drain excess oil. ● Enjoy warm.

绿豆馅麻团
SESAME BALLS WITH MUNG BEANS AND COCONUT

MAKES AROUND 12 PIECES

INGREDIENTS

SESAME SEEDS .... 1 CUP (150 G)
OIL FOR FRYING

FILLING

SPLIT YELLOW MUNG BEANS .... 1 CUP (200 G)
WHITE SUGAR .... ⅔ CUP (120 G)
GRATED COCONUT .... 1 CUP (50 G)
BUTTER .... 2⅓ TABLESPOONS
SALT .... 1 PINCH

DOUGH

GLUTINOUS (STICKY) RICE FLOUR .... 3⅓ CUPS (400 G)
+ A LITTLE TO WORK THE DOUGH
WHITE RICE FLOUR .... ¼ CUP (40 G)
BAKING POWDER .... 3 TEASPOONS
WHITE SUGAR .... ⅔ CUP (140 G)
SALT .... 1 PINCH
BOILING WATER .... 1½ CUPS (350 ML)

❶ Prepare the filling: soak the mung beans in a saucepan of cold water for 1 hour. ● Remove the water and pour in fresh water to ½ to ¾ inch (1 to 2 cm) above the level of the beans. ● Bring to a boil, then lower the heat and allow to simmer, stirring occasionally, until the liquid evaporates and the beans are cooked but not completely soft. ● Remove from the heat.

❷ Add the sugar and grated coconut to the pan. ● The mixture should have a chunky sauce-like consistency. ● Add the butter and salt, stir to combine, then place the mixture in the refrigerator.

❸ When the filling has firmed up and can be easily shaped, roll it into twelve 1 oz (25 g) balls, pressing firmly so they hold their shape. ● Set aside in the refrigerator for 1 hour.

❹ Prepare the dough by mixing the glutinous rice flour, rice flour, and baking powder in a bowl. ● Dissolve the sugar and salt in the boiling water. ● Gradually stir the water into the dry ingredients until combined. ● Knead until the dough is smooth.

❺ To shape dough balls, it is useful to have a small bowl of water and a small amount of glutinous rice flour nearby, in case the dough is very dry or very wet. ● Take 1¼ oz (35 g) dough and roll it into a ball, then flatten between your palms. ● Place a ball of cooled filling in the center, then wrap it completely with the dough. ● Try to keep an even thickness of dough around the ball to avoid having parts that are too thin and may burst during frying. Repeat with the remaining dough (you should end up with 12).

❻ When each ball is sealed, roll it in your hands to form a nice even ball, then coat with sesame seeds.

❼ Heat a 3 inch (8 cm) depth of oil in a deep pot to 300°F (150°C). Working in batches, fry the balls until they are nice and golden. ● Since they are quite dense, it is advisable to place a ball on a large slotted spoon, then lower it gently into the oil. ● A low temperature is recommended for frying so that the dough has time to cook before the outside becomes too crispy. ● Serve hot.

包
子
家
族

甜
点

拔丝苹果
APPLE FRITTERS
WITH CARAMEL

SERVES 2

INGREDIENTS

APPLES...2 LARGE
EGG WHITE ....FROM 2 EGGS (60 G)
SALT...1 PINCH
CORNSTARCH.............................½ CUP (60 G)

VEGETABLE OIL ....2 TEASPOONS + FOR FRYING
WHITE SUGAR ....½ CUP (100 G)
WATER ....⅓ CUP (80 ML)
ICE WATER TO SERVE

❶ Peel, core, and slice the apples into eighths, then cut each slice into 2 small pieces so you have small chunks.

❷ In a bowl, mix the egg white, salt, and cornstarch until a smooth, runny mixture is obtained, then pour in the 2 teaspoons of oil. ● Coat the apple pieces in the mixture.

❸ In a large pot, heat a 2 inch (5 cm) depth of oil to 325°F (160°C). ● Working in batches, fry the apple pieces until golden. ● Once cooked, transfer to paper towels to drain excess oil.

❹ In a saucepan or wok placed over medium heat, dissolve the sugar in the measured water. ● Allow to simmer gently until the syrup no longer contains water but before it caramelizes (at this stage, the syrup should crystallize and break easily once cooled).

❺ Add all the fried apple pieces to the wok or pan, then stir to coat each piece with syrup.

❻ Serve immediately in a bowl, accompanied by a small bowl of iced water. ● Dip the fried caramelized pieces in iced water to set the caramel and enjoy.

包
子
家
族

茶文化
TEA CULTURE

Legend has it that an Emperor discovered tea during a walk in 2737 BC and, ever since, consuming tea has become embedded in Chinese civilization and its traditions. Tea became an imperial drink from the eighth century onwards.

The tea tree was one of the first plants grown as a crop in China, in the region west of Yunnan. All types of tea (green, black, and white) come from the *Camellia sinensis* plant, but it is the way the leaves are harvested that determines the type.

Drinking tea has become an art and a state of mind. It symbolizes chan (*Zen*), self-control, hospitality, calm, refinement, and elegance. Tea houses opened and became places of community and sharing, as well as part of cultural life through displays of art, opera, and poetry. Drinking tea is a real experience in China; the quality of the tea is judged by its color, aroma, and flavor. The drinking experience is determined by the quality of the water and the teapot. The ceramics and porcelain used also impart the required aesthetic character to the experience.

HOW TO MAKE AND DRINK TEA

● High-quality teas are consumed without sugar, milk, or flavorings. ● All serveware (the teapot and cups) must be scalded before preparing the tea. ● Then the tea leaves are rinsed in hot water quickly before the first infusion, to wash them, but also to allow them to better develop their flavors. ● Water at the correct temperature is slowly poured over them. ● For green and white tea: 176–185°F (80–85°C) water is poured over 3 g tea leaves in a small teapot and infused for 3 to 5 minutes. ● For Oolong tea: 194–212°F (90–100°C) water is poured over 6 g tea leaves in a small clay teapot and infused for just 1 minute. ● For red tea: 194–203°F (90–95°C) water is poured over 6 g tea leaves in a 3½ cup (800 ml) teapot and infused for 3 to 5 minutes. ● For Pu-erh tea: 212°F (100°C) water is poured over 8 g tea leaves in a small clay teapot and infused for 2 minutes. ● It is possible to keep making up to five or even six successive infusions following the first one. Successive infusions are drunk in very small cups and at a fairly steady pace, a few sips each time. ● Choose a small-sized porcelain or Yixing clay teapot as the porosity of these pots retains the tea flavors. Ideally one teapot is designated to be used for each type of tea.

包
子
家
族

索引
INDEX

包子家族

包
子
家
族

鸣谢
ACKNOWLEDGEMENTS

This book is a crazy dream. The dream of sharing everything we love about Chinese cuisine and our traditions, through our eyes. This project is the result of six months' collaboration with passionate people, experts in their fields, who share our passion for cooking, travel, and creating hubs of urban life. *Bao Family Cookkbook* is a project close to my heart and I want to thank all the people who put their hearts and souls into the creation of this book:

— Authors Carole Cheung, Lynda Zhu.
— Bao Family chefs Lucy Chen, Jessica Chan, Victor Zheng, Liming Shu, Leslie Chirino, Tenzin Choeknor, Rachel Jiang, Alyssa Fowler, Andrej Demeter, Hong Hai Tran, Alex (Dorjee Lodoe Rabutsang), Madame Chun.
— My partner, Billy Pham, thank you for sharing this crazy adventure with me.
— All the Bao Family members who live out the Bao vibe every day.
— Donald Choque and Yoann Le Goff, our wonderful designers from Atelier Choque Le Goff for the artistic direction.
— Agathe Hernandez, our superb stylist, who went to Chinatown in Paris and Marseille to source the crockery.
— Grégoire Kalt, who brought his photographer's eye to our cooking.
— Catherine Roig and Lisa Grall, who made this book possible.
— And a special mention to the Bao Family members who make the Bao vibe come to life every day: Yana, Christian, Vann, Thavinh, Hanna, Ema, Simon, Laura, Léa, Guido, Caesar, Adrien, Aurélie, and all their teams.

包
子
家
族

BAO RESTAURANTS

Petit Bao 116 rue Saint Denis, 75002 Paris
Gros Bao 72 Quai de Jemmapes, 75010 Paris
Bleu Bao 8 rue Saint Lazare, 75009 Paris
Bao Express & Bao Bakery 10 rue Bréguet, 75011 Paris

....

First American edition published in 2023 by
Interlink Books
An imprint of Interlink Publishing Group, Inc.
46 Crosby Street
Northampton, Massachusetts 01060
www.interlinkbooks.com

Published simultaneously in the United
Kingdom and Australia by Murdoch Books,
an imprint of Allen & Unwin

First published in French in 2022 by
La Maison Hachette Pratique, an imprint
of Hachette Livre, France

Management: Catherine Saunier-Talec
Editorial Manager: Lisa Grall
Publisher Representative: Catherine Roig
Project Manager: Jeanne Mauboussin
Art direction and illustrations: Workshop
   Choque Le Goff, assisted by Cédric Houssen
Photography: Grégoire Kalt
Styling: Agathe Hernandez
Text preparation: Charlotte Müller
Layout: The Paoists
Production Manager: Amélie Latsch

Publisher: Céline Hughes
Translator: Nicola Thayil
English-language editor: Kay Halsey
American edition editor: Leyla Moushabeck
English-language designer and
   cover designer: Sarah McCoy

Library of Congress Cataloging-in-Publication Data available

ISBN 978-1-62371-742-1

Printed by C & C Offset Printing Co. Ltd., China

IMPORTANT: Those who might be at risk from the effects of salmonella poisoning (the
elderly, pregnant women, young children and those suffering from immune deficiency diseases)
should consult their doctor with any concerns about eating raw eggs. Please ensure that all
seafood and beef to be eaten raw or lightly cooked are very fresh and of the highest quality.

10 9 8 7 6 5 4 3 2 1

粤菜

GUANGDONG CUISINE

CHARACTERISTICS:
LIGHT, UMAMI, DELICATE, FRESH, SWEET

There are many cooking methods in Guangdong, or Cantonese, cuisine, which were adapted to use fresh ingredients and retain their natural flavors. Techniques include steaming, frying at high temperature, boiling, smothering, and wok-cooking. Spices and oil are used sparingly and dishes are not spicy so as to highlight the flavors of each ingredient. The most common seasonings used are cilantro, ginger, and pepper.

Cantonese cuisine is made up of Guangzhou cuisine, Chaoshan, or Teochew, cuisine and Hakka cuisine. Teochew cuisine is influenced by Fujian as well as Cantonese cuisine. It is present in Southeast Asia, as is Hakka cuisine due to migration. As they had to travel, the Hakka people attached more importance to the texture and taste of food than to its appearance. They also consumed a lot of dried and pickled foods.

川菜

SICHUAN CUISINE

CHARACTERISTICS:
RICH, HOT, SPICY, SWEET-AND-SOUR

Sichuan cuisine is the most popular cuisine in China. It is famous for being very spicy, although it should not be reduced to that.

As for cooking techniques, frying, steaming, and smothering are preferred. Pickled or smoked vegetables are also popular. Sichuan cuisine contains a lot of chiles, ginger, garlic, and Chinese five spice. Sichuan pepper, widely used in the region, imparts a tingly, numbing sensation to dishes—the hallmark of Sichuan cuisine. Spicy fermented bean sauce (dòu bàn jiàng, 豆瓣酱) is also a staple food. It is the combination of all these ingredients that gives dishes a flavorful and powerful taste.

苏菜

JIANGSU CUISINE

CHARACTERISTICS:
FRESH, DELICATE, LIGHT, UMAMI, SLIGHTLY SWEET

Jiangsu cuisine boasts over two millennia of history, yet it is probably the least known outside of China. The standard of living in the area is quite high, so the dishes often have a delicate appearance and use good-quality ingredients. Both saltwater and freshwater fish are common, and seasonal ingredients are preferred. Special attention is paid to preserving the natural flavors of the ingredients and to how they are cut. The most widely used cooking technique is stewing. Dishes have a combination of salty, umami, and slightly sweet flavors.

Jiangsu cuisine is made up of several styles, each often associated with a major city. Examples include Nanjing, Yangzhou, Suzhou, Huai'an, Xuzhou, and Haizhou cuisines.

浙菜

ZHEJIANG CUISINE

CHARACTERISTICS:
LIGHT, FRESH, DELICATE

The Zhejiang province is dominated by mountains and hills. It is one of the richest regions of China.

The cuisine of this region attaches great importance to the presentation of dishes. People enjoy using fresh produce, seafood, and seasonal vegetables. They consume a lot of raw or almost raw food, and the cooking techniques used are flash frying, wok-cooking, and steaming. Yellow rice wine is commonly used in seasonings and marinades.

Zhejiang cuisine can be divided into four major styles, each associated with one of the provincial cities: Shaoxing, whose wine is one of the best known varieties of yellow rice wine; Wenzhou; Ningbo, which focuses on the freshness and iodine taste of seafood, and is known for its pastry; and Hangzhou.